Off the Bridal Path
American Wedding
HUMOR

ANDERSON

NORDBOOK

For Adaire,

My Bride and Lover,

Who can make me laugh at

inappropriate times.

Introduction

After reading John Anderson's *Scandinavian Humor and Other Myths* and laughing loudly along the way, I was ready for *Off the Bridal Path*. Every bride and groom will recognize themselves in this very funny book which examines every aspect of weddings, from why people get married to what it will be like celebrating your anniversary in the twenty-first century.

I predict this book will be a great gift – just the thing to help a couple preserve their sanity throughout the wedding process.

Read it, enjoy, keep laughing...I do.

Mary Hart
Entertainment Tonight

Other books by John Louis Anderson:
Scandinavian Humor & Other Myths
German Humor: On the Fritz

John Louis Anderson has been behaving like a newlywed since September 7, 1974, when he married the world's most nearly perfect person, Adaire Colleen Peterson.

Since then, he has published the best-selling *Scandinavian Humor & Other Myths* and *German Humor; On the Fritz*. He was born and raised in New Ulm, Minnesota, where he got his professional introduction to weddings at Oswald Studio. He has worked as a photographer for the Guthrie Theater and a number of national magazines and advertising agencies in the United States and Europe. Mr. Anderson does not do weddings.

First Printing......................................January 1993
Published by
NORDBOOK, INC.
P.O. Box 249
Chaska, MN 55318

Library of Congress Cataloging in Publication Data
Anderson, John Louis
Off the Bridal Path: American Wedding Humor
1 United States – Marriage Customs and Social Life
– Anecdotes, humor, etc.

ISBN 0-9616967-2-9

Text, photography and hand tinting:
John Louis Anderson
Editor:
Sylvia Paine
Cover and text design:
Yamamoto Moss
Printing:
Gopher State Litho
Separations:
Professional Litho

Table of Contents

The
Wedding of
Our Darling
Daughter
to
What's-His-Name

Weddings/engagements

F. Clark Burgess's Daughter Marries Law Student

Missi Burgess, the daughter of F. Clark and Bea Burgess, was married to Marc Taylor, son of Ray Taylor and the former Mrs. (Sunny) Taylor at the House of Appropriate Behavior Presbyterian Church last Saturday.

Marc is a third-year law student at the University Law School and is the winner of the "Moot Court-Outstanding Damage Award in a Medical Malpractice Case" student competition.

Missi is an undergraduate student of interior design and an aerobics instructor at "Pretty/Sweaty," the popular workout studio. The bride wore a white satin gown with re-embroidered lace overlays and a cathedral train. The maid of honor was Traci Burgess, the bride's sister, and the attendants were Betsi Quaintance, Marci Shatter and Kelli Krekelberg. All four women, who wore matching teal green long-sleeve lace dresses with satin trim, are charter members of Brownie Troop 351. Mrs. Burgess wore a peachy-salmon tea-length pleated poly-blend dress with matching shoes and hose. Carissa Wudel was the flower girl and Nicholas Burgess would have been the ring boy if he had been prepared to act like a gentleman.

The best man was Troy "Doozie" Bang, who, like the rest of the groom's party, is a member of the Barrister Bombers, the law-school softball team. The groomsmen were Peter Titze (team equipment manager), Alec van Buskirk (outfield), Todd Bickett (first base) and Brandon McAllister (catcher). F. Clark Burgess, the bride's father, is a local real-estate developer and owner of several nursing homes. Mrs. Burgess is the president of the local chapter of P.M.S. (Prevent Musical Smut).

Ray Taylor, the groom's father, the president of Taylor/Kravis/LaBree Advertising, which specializes in lottery promotions, was accompanied by his new wife, Geri, who wore an ivory and green side-draped, shirred-torso mat-jersey dress identical to the one worn by Mr. Taylor's first wife, Sunny. Neither woman was available for comment.

I'll Always Love Dadd[y]
Who was my first hero
Who taught me all I knew,
My Daddy, that's who!

Who was there to cheer me
When I was sad and blue,
My Daddy, that's who!

Who was my first boyfriend,
To whom my little thoughts flew,
My Daddy, that's who!

Soon I will be married
And your mission will be through,
Daddy, It's You!!!

Brides are Happy Girls!

I feel so pretty in these
pictures— my wedding day
was such a SPECIAL Day + I
felt so special + pretty all
day, because it was my
special day!

I'm special 'cuz I'm a Bride!

Mom gets along a little better with Marc now, but last Christmas was something else!

Happy Holidays

BEA & F. CLARK

req...

at th...

P...

son of Mr. and ...

on **Saturday**,

at **3** o...

Bevins Creek Metho...

Bevins Creek, Min...

Carl Krekelberg

of your presence

heir daughter

Wudel

er 17

I'm special 'cuz I'm a Bride!

Who would
have believed
that all my
little cousins
would come to
my special day?

I'm special 'cuz I'm a Bride!

Keli had to move
her wedding because
it was the same
day as mine, but
she already had the
invitations printed—
so—she just took
white-out & typed over
them! CAN you BELIEVE her!?!

MARC AND MISSI

Marc and Missi

Brides are Happy Girls!
Not only did Marc's Dad bring that new Yuppie Hussy of his, but she wore the same dress Marc's Mom did! And Marc didn't seem to even care that my special day would be RUINED!

Come to a
"Naughty"
&
...ce"

...ower
for Missi!

...k and lacy is "wicked,"
...owave-ware makes dinner "snappy!"
...rl needs them both
...keep her man "happy"!

Brides are Happy Girls!
Aunt Sandra & Aunt Lois
were at it again! I spent $2575.56
on my own gown and all they could
do was criticize! I honestly don't
think those old women know how
much a wedding costs now days!
If they did, they wouldn't be so
mean!!

I'm special 'cuz I'm a Bride!
Poor Grandma! Because of all of the Shortages during the War, she could only have one attendant!

I'm special 'cuz I'm a Bride!
Leave it to Doozie!

* First, he hand-cuffed Marc and then lost the key.... * then
* he snuck up on us when we were getting dressed......

I'm special 'cuz I'm a Bride!
Dad's SO funny! Whenever anyone asked him what the wedding COST, he just pulled out his pockets & made a face!

I'm special 'cuz I'm a Bride!

Are we ready
for MTV
or what?

Happy 16 Month Anniversary
I LOVE YOU!
I LOVE YOU!
I LOVE YOU!
I LOVE YOU!

I'm special 'cuz I'm a Bride!
Marc was so sweet to make an appointment with that independent Cosmetology technician and get me such good skin lotion!

Brides are Happy Girls!
Marc was picking frosting out of his nose for three days!! (I loved every minute of it.)
The champagne fountains in the cake were just the perfect touch! Everybody was jealous!

I'm special 'cuz I'm a Bride!
Dad just had to show everyone all my baby pictures!

I'm special 'cuz I'm a Bride!
Everyone acted like it was my fault that the bouquet went so far — I can't help it if Aunt Sara is so COMPETETIVE!

I can't believe that Marc thought it would be funny to take off my garter with his teeth!

I'm special 'cuz I'm a Bride!
Uncle Harry was certainly color coordinated for the day!

Las Vegas Night-Lites

I'm special 'cuz I'm a Bride!
Las Vegas is SO ROMANTIC and ^{so} Glamorous!

Barker & Muffy had their own Special Day!

So true!

YOUR LOVE LIFE WILL BE
HAPPY AND FULFILLING.

A THRILLING TIME IS IN
YOUR IMMEDIATE FUTURE.

BABY
ON
BOARD!

I'm special 'cuz I'm a Bride!
Weddings are
hard on the feet
but they're good
for the soles!
(DAD told me that!
He's such a stitch!)

THE NIGHT GRANDMA HAD AN AUTO-BODY EXPERIENCE

Most brides don't really believe that their mother ever had sex, and the idea of Grandma pointing her toes is more than most twentysomethings can even comprehend. But some things never change. When people are madly in love, sex happens – always has and always will.

You can be sure that Grandma spent her youth exploring the outer limits of respectability, and you can be absolutely certain that your great-grandmother had a conniption fit when Sheriff Swansson told her what he found!

Why People Get Married

*P*eople get married because they're so madly in love that they want to live with this person for the rest of their lives and share 14 percent mortgages and cats who need surgery and children who need braces.

You say that you're madly in love and want to get married. Let's sit down and examine your reasons. There are good reasons and bad reasons to get married. A good reason to get married is that you will never again have to walk back to your apartment alone at 3 A.M. in a January blizzard. A bad reason to get married is that your job is really, *really* boring.

In prehistoric times, unmarried people had to live on the outskirts of the village, where they would be more likely to be eaten by lions or bears.

This provided a strong motivation to get married. Nowadays, it's the married people who live in the suburbs and the single people live in the urban centers where there are restaurants that serve calamari appetizers and nobody will give you a loan for a house – unless you're married or have two incomes in an arrangement your mother doesn't want to talk about.

It's best to marry early in life because people who live on their own too long get so set in their ways that only the most overwhelming passion will enable them to share the same house with someone else. This chapter examines that special period after you kick out your roommate and discover you can't afford the apartment by yourself, but before you fall in love with someone.

Should You Get Married?

*N*ot everyone should get married. In fact, a whole lot of people shouldn't even be dating, let alone picking out Melmac patterns for a gift registry. How do you know if you're one of these people? Here's a quick test:

1. Do you stop a doubles tennis game to instruct your partner on his/her backhand?
2. Do you expect to settle down and have kids as soon as you find someone as attractive as you?
3. Do you correct other people's grammar or pronunciation?
4. Do you find that you have to do most of the talking on dates because other people are so seldom articulate?
5. Do you break the ice on first dates by talking about what a wonderful cook, homemaker, parent, etc., your mother is?
6. Do you rearrange everyone's silverware at a dinner party if the hostess set the table wrong?
7. Do you audibly say "E-flat!" when your eight-year-old nephew flubs a note at his piano recital?
8. If you are caught outdoors at sunset, do you dismiss the whole display as "cheap middle-class sentimentality!"?
9. Do you manage to bring the name of your prestigious alma mater into contexts others might not have anticipated?
10. Do you believe there are many people who need you more than you need them?

If you answered yes to any of these questions, you might not want to get married. If you answered yes to many questions, you're probably so self-sufficient that you don't need much mortal contact at all.

That just leaves the rest of us trying to find a sane and sexy date in a world full of crazies, where foreplay now includes getting tested. There are some warning signs you should know. If you ever find yourself in any of these situations, do not panic. Slowly back out of the room, walk calmly to your car and lock the doors.

Then panic.

Dating Danger Signs for Women

1. Is there a police scanner radio in his apartment, and does he shout advice to it?
2. Does he get angry if you lean against his car because your coat has a zipper and zippers can scratch?
3. Is his bathtub full of newspapers, beer cans or books?
4. Does he have a dog or cat that looks like something out of an Edgar Allan Poe story?
5. Does he admit to getting into fights, but insists that somebody else made him do it - every time?
6. Does he refuse to answer the doorbell whenever there's a ball game on cable TV?
7. Do you think of him as a brooding hunk, while your friends just think he's psychotic?
8. Does he try to impress you by telling you that he's a gourmet cook and that Maserati is his favorite Italian cheese?
9. Does he talk a lot about "pushy women" and suggest that any woman who won't have sex with him is a lesbian?
10. Does he assure you he can handle it every time he has a drink, even though you haven't said anything?

Dating Danger Signs for Men

1. Does she wear a Harley Davidson tube top and a rhinestone necklace that says, "Damn, I'm Good"?
2. Does she already have an extensive collection of "Precious Moments" statuettes, even though she's only twenty-three years old?
3. Does she have the entire Time-Life series on the occult, and are her responses always late, as if she were on a two-second tape delay?
4. Just before you make love for the first time, does she tell you, "No one has ever been able to satisfy me"?
5. Does she tell you that you can learn valuable psychology lessons by watching soap operas?
6. Are all her ex-boyfriends dead or in prison?
7. Are the ones in prison due to be released soon?
8. Does she think an R-rating means a movie is filthy and disgusting?
9. Does she describe everything she likes as "cute"?
10. Does she spend the entire first date talking about how much fun it is to be around babies?

Understanding Your Partner

*A*s soon as you decide to get married, you will discover that marriage is life's way of proving how opposite the opposite sex can be. Luckily, marriage is not a class-action suit, and you are not marrying *all* women or *all* men, just one isolated example. Just how isolated depends on your tastes, of course, but you should remember that if you have to dress up like a French maid to get his attention, things are only going to get stranger.

Men and women evolved separately, men from reptiles (which explains why Sumo wrestlers and lizards walk so much alike) and women from birds (where the instinct to feather the nest has devolved into evening crafts classes).

Here are some other valuable anthropological tidbits to help you understand your potential partner.

Men are more loyal than women. They are loyal to old friends whom they no longer like, because men form hierarchies while women form alliances.

Women prefer a loose web of alliances because they realize that both things and people change. Men think shifting alliances seem unfair, like moving second base after the runner has started. In a hierarchy, relationships are clearly defined and relatively constant. Your job is to be loyal to those relationships.

Men are even loyal to inanimate objects, like leather goods, and that's where the *real* trouble begins. No woman can understand why a man would be loyal to a billfold until it mildews and falls apart. On average, one, maybe two billfolds will last a man from his wedding day to his grandchild's college graduation. Women, on the other hand, buy, use and discard purses before the leather gets its first scratch. Men see this as a shocking display of disloyalty to an old friend. A wife typically dismisses her husband's touching loyalty to his wallet as proof that he is just as stingy as his father. Luckily for men, women are more loyal to their husbands than they are to their purses, or there would have to be lots of support groups for lonely guys showing each other old wallets.

Women court pneumonia waving their fingers out of a car window to dry a new coat of fingernail polish. This might be all right when they are alone but riding with a polish drier in January can be downright hazardous. Men are more rational, and only stick their hands out of car windows to make airplane wings, scientifically proving that the principles of lift and drag are still in effect.

Men throw food into their mouths in an ancient male bonding ritual designed to prove their marksmanship. This trait dates to Neolithic times, when a young boy would have to prove his hunting skills by spearing a saber-toothed tiger before he could squat and scratch around the campfire with the men.

Men think that breaking wind is funny. Worse yet, they consider it a uniquely male form of nonverbal communication. This also dates back to the Lower Neolithic Age, when talking was taboo on the great mastodon hunts because it would spook the mastodons, who didn't talk, although they did break wind. At least the male mastodons did.

Machismo is genetically programmed behavior. In animals, it's called display behavior, and it involves butting heads with other males, roaring at intruders and marking one's territory in irritating ways. The difference between human machismo and animal display behavior is that male animals display only to other males, while human males direct this aggression toward women, who don't enjoy butting heads for entertainment.

Living in Sin: A Fresh Look

A wedding is what results when parents get involved with your plans to live with someone. That's called the Push Factor. The Pull Factor refers to all the goodies you get from your friends and relatives.

The big problem with living in sin is that nobody rewards that sort of behavior with gifts. Most young couples *need* those towels, sheets, frying pans and salad shooters. After all, a yogurt maker can be returned to the store for cash.

The alternative is to plug along using the junk you've already got in your apartments. You know, his threadbare Spuds MacKenzie towels and your tablecloth with the pumpkin ooze marks left from your first Halloween together, when he carved a pumpkin and you left it on the table till it decomposed.

But with the rise of two-income couples and the disintegration of the nuclear family (which typically has a half-life of only one argument), the old Push Factor is not as ominous as it used to be.

It's time we took a fresh look at what used to be called living in sin. It's got to be better than dying in divorce court.

Benefits to Living in Sin:

1. You and your mother will have something to talk about every time you meet for the next decade.
2. You don't have to plan or finance a wedding.
3. In fifteen years, there won't be a whole album of pictures of you in funny clothes and a weird hair-do.
4. You won't have to write thank-you notes.
5. Every day that God doesn't strike you dead will be a thorn in the side of hypermoral coworkers.
6. You won't have to diet for three months to fit into your gown.
7. There will be absolutely no pressure on you from your family to have lots of babies, quickly.
8. Nobody will try to sell you life insurance on the phone once you tell them that you're just living together.
9. You will have a clearer idea of what belongs to whom, so it will be easier to divide your property if you split up.
10. You won't have in-laws who expect you to show up for family events. In fact, your partner's parents will be quietly grateful if you don't.

Something Old, Something New: Prenuptial Contracts

A lot has been made recently of the prenuptial contracts of the very rich and anal-retentive. Sums that most of us can't comprehend are tossed about as if they were deserved. It's just proof that in America anyone can rise to the top, but when they do they'll probably get divorced and have low-lifes like us reading their 1040 forms in the tabloids.

Most of us will never have enough money to make our divorce amusing to strangers, but that doesn't mean we shouldn't consider prenuptial contracts. The value of a contract is not to provide an end point to a relationship but to provide a framework for making a partnership work.

What more could anyone want as they set out in marriage? A contract offers a clearly defined set of expectations, a minimum level of accountability and perhaps a provision for merit pay. You could even write in a sunset clause to keep the other party on his or her toes. Then review the contract every five years to determine compliance and make continuation of the contract contingent upon the fulfillment of these criteria. Ruthless, yes – but how is America ever going to regain its lead against foreign competitors unless we take decisive action on the home front?

For those small entrepreneurial/nuptial organizations being started every day, here are some guidelines for preliminary contracts.

Standard Male Marriage Contract

I, _____, being of sound mind and fevered body, am about to marry _____, and do agree to these minimum standards for my marriage:

- I will cook as often as I did for myself before I got married without making her feel like I'm doing her this big favor.
- I will spend more time with her than I do with the guys without making her feel like I'm doing her this big favor.
- I will do my share of keeping the stuff picked up in my house without making her feel like I'm doing her this big favor.
- If I find that I am totally incapable and/or unreliable in the above, I will hire a cleaning service and pay for it myself.

- ♨ I will fight fairly and not say "I don't care" or go totally silent.
- ♨ The only mind games I will play on her will be "peek-a-boo," and only immediately preceding sex.
- ♨ I will follow the minimum standards of personal hygiene as set down in the Boy Scout handbook, fantasizing, if I must, that showering daily is as rugged as bathing in an icy mountain stream.
- ♨ I will make no jokes about her relatives, who are no weirder than mine, only different.
- ♨ I will not compare her to former lovers – romantically, intellectually, socially or in physical appearance.
- ♨ I will not form emotional attachments to torn, shrunken, pilled or frayed clothing, nor will I wear my clothes past their freshness date.

Signed _____

Witness _____

Standard Female Marriage Contract

I, _____, being of sound mind and fevered body, am about to marry _____, and do agree to these minimum standards for my marriage:

- ♨ I will have headaches only when my head aches, not when I do not want to be touched.
- ♨ I will fight fairly and not whine or cry.
- ♨ I will not blame all of our children's bad character traits on my husband's admittedly odd family.
- ♨ I will strive mightily to enjoy his hobbies and sports, although it is understood that he will clean his own fish.
- ♨ I will not secretly discard old articles of his clothing without first calling an emergency session of the Family Council to debate the topic.
- ♨ I will not unfairly use my superior female language skills to win family arguments by confusing him. We will play Paper/Stone/Scissors, going two out of three for really serious philosophical debates.
- ♨ I will not put my pantyhose in the washing machine with his underwear so that it wraps and knots everything together.
- ♨ I will not threaten that if he's not nice to me now, I will get back at him when I get PMS and nobody will convict me.
- ♨ I will not point out that he has all of his father's bad habits and darned few of his good ones.
- ♨ I will never tell him what my mother said about him the first time she met him.

Signed _____

Witness _____

The Prince and the Gypsy Contract

We've all heard the fairy tale about the prince or princess who runs away with the poor but charming gypsy. The hilarious moral of the story is that the prince(ss) gives up the throne and discovers the joy of honest, backbreaking labor in badly lit factories to be with the love of his (her) life.

In the late twentieth century, very rich men – generally speaking – are not so delusional that they believe that multiorgasmic young women seek them out for their bodies. Very rich women, on the other hand, sometimes *do* flatter themselves that handsome young men with no visible means of support are attracted by their minds.

You may already be in love with someone who's filthy rich, but it's no coincidence that you haven't been made a cosigner on his or her safe deposit box. This means there's a contract in your future. Your only choice is whose: your contract or your partner's? The first rule is never to sign a contract offered by somebody else's lawyer. Signing somebody else's contract is like agreeing to pay somebody else's alimony. And not to put too fine a point on it, but it's *your* alimony we're talking about here!

The "I am not a Boy-Toy" Contract

(Circle as many as may be applicable)

I, _____, am marrying _____ because:

A) I really respect her mind;   B) she's kind to 1. animals 2. small children 3. me; and

C) we share deeply held beliefs about 1. animal rights; 2. personal growth; 3. deforestation of the rain forest;

4. the healing power of crystals; 5. other – (please specify)_____,

I want nothing more than to spend my life running my fingers through her:

1. long; 2. short; 3. curly; 4. other_____ ; 5. blonde; 6. brunette; 7. black; 8. other_____ hair, gazing into her: 9. blue; 10. brown; 11. black; 12. grey–green; 13. other_____ eyes and managing her personal affairs and career.

I declare that although I may have loved others before (see attached Agenda A) they are as but the chaff in the wind to me now. My all-consuming love for _____ is so pure that I can think of nothing else till she doth wed to me and I was totally unaware that she was filthy rich until she brought it up just this very minute. Honest to God!

Date _____	Witness	_____
Signed _____	Witness	_____
Notarized _____	Witness	_____

The "I am not a Bimbo" Contract
(Circle as many as may be applicable)
I, _____, do solemnly swear that the only reason I am marrying _____ is that:
A) his powerful, masculine body drives me insane with desire:
B) he is as vigorous as a man half his age;
C) he is a caring individual who will take time away from his business interests to be with me.

All I ask is to be by his side, to tell him how wonderful and wise he is and to make him feel good about himself even when he is under a lot of stress from the:

1. bankers; 2. regulators; 3. Justice Department; 4. stockbrokers; 5. shareholders; 6. IRS; 7. liberal press.

In the event our union should ever dissolve, I would be too heartbroken to make any financial demands upon him, wanting nothing more than to have him return once again to my bosom.

To prepare for his eventual return, I would, however, need to meet certain reasonable expenses to maintain myself in the manner to which he has become accustomed. (See attached Agenda A)

Date _____   Witness _____
Signed _____   Witness _____
Notarized _____   Witness _____

"You're What?" Romantic Ways of Popping the Question

The marriage proposal is the man's only major contribution to the wedding festivities. Everything else is done by and for women. This is the guy's chance to be a knight in shining armor, even if the shining armor has to be back at the costume rental shop tomorrow.

Men: Seize the opportunity! Make it memorable! This is your chance to be a superstar! Timing, of course, is everything. If you aren't careful, the woman may force the issue with a little announcement of her own, which could reduce your options to: "You're what? Well, I suppose..."

Some guys propose with style. Robbin Dokken had always told Jim Brandli that she thought he was a knight in shining armor, so Jim rented some gladiator armor (wrong period, but hey, armor is armor) and found a clear plastic shoe, which is as close to a glass slipper as you're going to get today. His white charger was an old mare, which was fine with him because he had never been on a horse in his life. The lady fair accepted his gallant proposal in front of the Y Motel, and they strolled – not rode – off to their own Camelot.

Dale Gross's proposal had fireworks. *Was* fireworks, to be exact. Inspired by the opening of the old TV Show *Love, American Style*, this fireworks crew member designed a rack of fireworks that read "Marry me, Lisa," and ignited it during the Fourth of July fireworks display. He had just enough fireworks saved to set off the "Y" in Marry, the "E" in me, and the "S" in Lisa, so the audience wouldn't be kept in suspense as to her reply. She accepted.

Sports scoreboards are a peculiarly male form of communication. Mike Kelly proposed to Kim Cendening on the scoreboard at a hockey game. The organist played the wedding march, the scoreboard flashed "Will You Marry Me?" and the TV cameras zoomed in on her (she was *quite* surprised). She accepted, he slipped a ring on her finger, and the scoreboard flashed "YES," as the crowd roared.

One Sunday while everybody else was in church, John Anderson plowed "MARRY ME SHIRLEY" in 40-foot-wide letters, a half-mile long and a quarter-mile wide. Then he casually took Shirley Bauer up in his single-engine plane to look at the fall colors. She must have enjoyed the colors immensely because he finally had to turn the plane on its side for her to see the proposal. It took a few minutes for it to sink in. Eventually she realized she hadn't given him an answer, so she accepted and suggested that they land real soon since she was "a little queasy from all that excitement."

The danger with a public proposal is that it can go terribly wrong. There's always the possibility the woman will say, "Well, let me get back to you on that…" More likely, though, she simply might not *see* it. She'll get up and go to the bathroom just before the scoreboard flashes, or she'll get airsick.

One fellow took extra pains to assure that his intended got his message. In a guest editorial in the Fourth of July edition of the local newspaper, Stephen MacLennan wrote of his gratitude for his country's liberal refugee policy, which enabled him to meet Mai Ta when she came to attend college. Then, right there in front of God, the public and the copy editors, he proposed.

The problem was that Mai Ta subscribed to a different newspaper. So he covered his bases by writing "My dearest Mai, will you marry me?" on a scrap of paper, stuffing it into a pop bottle and "hiding" it in bushes near a lake.

Then he had to get her to walk around the lake, convince her to help him pick up "litter" and make sure she picked up the right bottle. She picked it up, but it took a lot of prodding to get her to pull out the scrap of paper. *Finally* she pulled out the message, he pulled a diamond ring from his pocket and his proposal was complete. Whew!

Another drawback to public proposals is the attention you'll get if you haven't been behaving yourself. In one case, it wasn't the proposal but the best man's prank announcement on a billboard: "AFTER AUGUST 23rd THE STREETS WILL BE SAFE. John Goodman is getting married."

His friends couldn't believe that he was going to settle down, and even his fiancée described him as a "three-girls-a-night-big-bachelor." When the billboard appeared, the local paper ran an amusing article, which drew the attention of an unamused former secretary who had filed a sexual-harassment case against Goodman for being what they used to call "persistent."

Some people are better off keeping a low profile.

Doing the Right Thing

Getting married should not be a selfish action taken just to please yourself and your partner. That's what fooling around is for. Marriage serves many important purposes, such as keeping your grandmother's heart from being broken and letting your mother stage the wedding she really wanted when she got married.

Getting married is the ultimate in unselfishness, for you turn your life over to strangers as soon as you announce your engagement. Everybody gets a part of you. Your mother takes the wedding, grandmothers call all the relatives, aunts schedule showers, caterers demand you pick a menu, and so on.

Why do people go through all this trouble when they could just get married on a Harley-Davidson at the Sturgis motorcycle rally? Because they have a moral responsibility to their friends and family to provide opportunities to gossip and pass judgment.

The nuclear family is an underemployed resource constantly looking for work. Weddings are a perfect chance for everybody to pull together, if only so they can be within hitting range of each other.

Families nowadays gather only at weddings and funerals, and people are often, but not always, in better moods at the weddings.

Surviving Marital Peer Pressure

Some people get married because they think their friends expect them to. You might be surprised to learn that only about forty percent of a woman's friends and seven percent of a man's friends are even aware of whom they're dating, let alone whether they're serious enough to consider marriage. Men know their friends' self-destructive tendencies, so instead of a moral tirade when the news of the break-up comes, a typical male conversation runs like this:

Friend: "You still seeing, ah, you-know...?

You: "Nah..."

Friend: "Oh."

Because relationships are important to women, they try to keep a break-up secret so their friends won't pity-bomb them. But women also believe that Talking About It is important, so their conversation sounds more like this:

Friend: "You still dating Jim, the musician with the brown hair and glasses?

You: "Well...not really..."

Friend: "What a rat."

Friend #2: "You poor thing! Tell us all about it."

Friend #3: "I never did trust him!"

And you're off! By the end of the evening, you'll feel like you just escaped marrying a serial killer.

Bad (and Some Good) Reasons to Get Married

There are hundreds of good reasons to get married, most of which are catalogued monthly in various women's magazines. Of course, the magazines don't mention the best reasons, like having someone to blame when you can't find your keys, or having a ready excuse to avoid dull parties ("Sounds like a great time! Let me check with my wife and see what she's got planned...").

With so many great reasons to get married, why do people continue to marry for the worst of reasons? Probably because they want to get married in the worst possible way, and lord, how they do succeed!

Bad Reasons for Women to Get Married

1. He's rich.
2. He's popular.
3. You can't stand living with your family one more day.
4. All your friends expect you to get married.
5. He's the only man you've met since moving here four years ago.
6. Your job is boring.
7. Your friends say you're a cute couple.
8. Everybody says you'd have really cute kids.
9. You don't know how else you could have sex.
10. He has this really great car.
11. Your ex- (boyfriend or husband) hates him.
12. You feel kind of sorry for him.
13. You can help change his life for him.
14. It may be your last chance.
15. You're lonely.
16. He'll always take care of you.
17. He says no one besides him could ever love you.
18. Even though he always seems to be hurting you, you've been with him so long that there's no point in leaving now.
19. Your mother thinks he's great.
20. Your father thinks he's a bad influence.

Bad Reasons for Men to Get Married

1. Why not?
2. Your friends think she's hot stuff.
3. You'll get unlimited sex for the rest of your life.
4. You guess it's a good idea.
5. She really wants to get married.
6. She could really help you with your career.
7. She needs someone to take care of her.
8. She's cute and perky.
9. She was Miss Teen New Jersey a few years back.
10. She's not one of those ball-busting feminists. *You'll* be making all the decisions around here.
11. A man's home is his castle and every castle needs a queen.
12. She drinks less than you do.
13. You've been going together since eighth grade.

What would people think if you broke up now?

14. She'll help you settle down.
15. You want someone to look after you when you're eighty.
16. She doesn't have anybody to look after her.
17. Her dad will give you a soft job at his company.
18. She always stayed with you even though you hurt her. You feel like you sort of owe it to her.
19. Your father thinks she's great.
20. Your mother thinks she's awful.

"That's fine," you say, "But I'm just illogical sometimes, I'm not pathological. Let's hear the good reasons for getting married."

The problem is that all the best reasons are so profoundly personal that you'd no more talk about them than you'd talk about your bedroom kinks. What's more, these reasons are just *dripping* with sincerity and it's boring as hell listening to someone talk about being soulmates.

Still, lurking behind the gush are some darned good practical reasons for getting married. Let's examine a few.

Good Reasons for Anyone to Get Married

1. You'll have someone to blame when you can't find your keys.
2. You'll always have someone to tell you what you did wrong at the party and how much it embarrassed everyone.
3. You'll always have a date for the State Fair.
4. You'll have an excellent source of and audience for gossip.
5. You can do a Good Cop/Bad Cop number on your household pets.
6. You'll have someone to pamper you when you have a cold or the flu. To a point, at least.
7. Your spouse will validate your suspicion that your family really is weird and you're not crazy for thinking that.
8. You'll have someone to help you "de-": de-brief, de-compress and sometimes de-toxify.
9. You have someone who will argue with you at the drop of a hat until your children are teenagers and take over that responsibility.
10. There is no technology equal to the small of your sweetie's back for warming up cold toes on a midwinter night.

YOU WONDER HOW THESE THINGS BEGIN...

Many women begin planning their weddings early. Some begin in preschool. Barbie Weddings are pure fantasy, unbounded by economic necessity or cultural history – a perfect metaphor for American weddings.

For a Barbie Wedding you need a Barbie, a Barbie Wedding dress, a Barbie maid of honor and maybe a Ken. If you can't find a Ken, My Little Pony can stand in for him. It's all the same to a little girl.

As girls grow older, they move from playing Big Barbie Wedding to playing Barbie Divorce and Second Wedding – which is even more wonderful and thrilling than the first, because Barbie has finally found the only man she could ever truly love.

Preparing for the Perfect Wedding

*W*e give weddings to show people what we want to be, not what we are. We want to be rich, young, thin, desirable and doubt-free. We want to be *perfect!*

But perfection is a bright and shining lie. Your wedding is supposed to be *perfect!* It's your *perfect* day! Your gown has to be *perfect,* the flowers have to be *perfect,* the catering has to be *perfect,* the music has to be *perfect,* the groom has to be...well, nobody talks about grooms that way.

The months before a wedding can be the most exciting in a woman's life. Certainly they will be the busiest. Not until she has a baby will a woman receive so much attention again. This is why you shouldn't be pregnant when you get married – you'll waste two parties by combining them.

Don't rush the engagement period. Putting on a wedding is a big business, similar to an unfriendly takeover of a major oil company. You'll need time to work out the details. This is when you make those interesting little discoveries about your future spouse, such as that he eats with his fingers *all the time*, or that she intends to put dust ruffles on *all* the furniture. In short, this is when you panic.

As usual, women get to have the most fun during this time – sleeping in hand-lotioned body stockings to make their skin as soft as a southern belle's and going to showers where they can play "Fish Pond" with their mother's friends.

So relax and remember that no one makes it through this period with her dignity intact.

What's Going on in Your Future Spouse's Head Anyway?

Women marry thinking they can change their husbands. Men marry thinking their wives will never change. Both are wrong. All you can hope for is to understand your spouse.

Men and women are equally crazy, but they're crazy in different ways, which is what makes the opposite sex such an irritating novelty. For example, it's easier for a woman to spend two years in therapy learning about her deepest fears than it is for her to learn what her husband wants to do this weekend.

Women and men are socialized differently (when men are socialized at all). Each has identifiable patterns. Studying these patterns will help you understand your sweetie and may even help protect your fanny in some tight spots.

Interpretation of the Female Chart

Fear of Loneliness

The largest lobe in the female brain concerns itself with the fear of loneliness. As a rule, men are largely insensitive to loneliness except on Saturday nights and at the onset of the Empty Nest Syndrome. Women, on the other hand, realize that loneliness is what life is all about. This is why women dance together at high school dances and why women have friends while men have business associates. It may explain why women have children. It certainly explains why some women will marry nearly anything in the vain hope that they will not be lonely.

Relationships

Much has been written about male bonding, but the hard fact is that women are better at bonding than men. Women cherish and nurture their relationships. They work hard at them, seeking consensus, patching up misunderstandings and soothing old wounds. Men's attitude about relationships is "If they can't take a joke, flick 'em." Women's relationships provide them with useful stuff such as gossip, restaurant reviews and unsolicited advice on how to raise their children. Men bond only to kill something: ducks, time or a bottle.

Good Manners

There is a special good-manners lobe in women's brains that keeps them from being as slovenly as men. This lobe prevents women from spitting out of car windows, breaking wind in public or becoming world-class belchers. It has no connection whatsoever with knowing how to properly and politely answer an engraved invitation, with writing thank-you notes or any other learned (or unlearned) behavior. It may have something to do with animal rights.

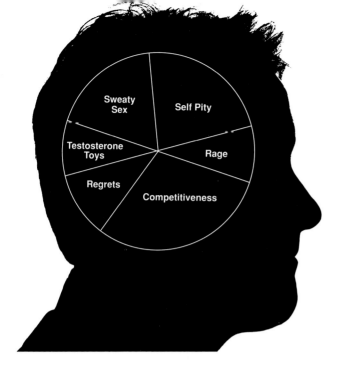

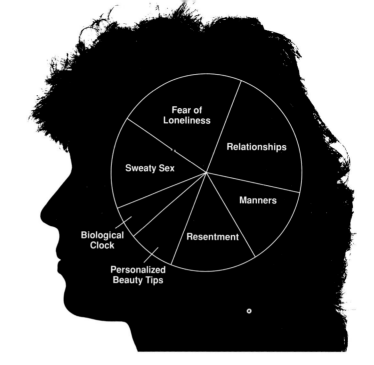

Resentment

Because women have such good manners, they also have twelve full place settings of resentment. Resentment is ambition choked by politeness. Men's idea of being polite is never to hurt anyone unintentionally. The closest men come to resentment is jealousy, which is love poisoned by impotence.

Personalized Beauty Tips, New Design Ideas, 12 Exciting Dishes You Can Make With Zucchini, and Pasta Diets.

The so-called "magazine section" of a woman's brain is crammed with exciting articles such as "How To Make Your Orgasms Burn Cellulite." As a woman ages, the composition of this section changes from articles like "Mental Health through Mutual Orgasm" in *Cosmopolitan* to articles from the *Reader's Digest* about horrible new diseases that anyone can catch.

Biological Clock

Generally speaking, women want babies. They attribute this lust to reproduce to their biological clock, a tiny gland which, when stimulated by the fear of loneliness in old age, produces an annoying ringing in some people's ears. In some women, the biological clock more closely resembles a biological time bomb, a device that can go off unexpectedly anytime from junior high onwards. Men have a biological clock too, but it's more like a stopwatch.

Sweaty Sex

There's no doubt that women like sweaty sex as much as men do, although some prefer Amway parties. Women believe that good sweaty sex requires foreplay. Sex for them is like aerobics. While men will go jogging in any old gym shorts they can find, women painstakingly shop for matching Lycra exercise suits, acquire attractive warm-up jackets and sometimes even find smear-proof make-up for the event. Women are divided as to what constitutes adequate foreplay. Some are content with what amounts to a formal introduction, while others are unsatisfied if foreplay doesn't begin as early as last New Year's Eve.

Interpretation of the Male Chart

Rage

It's seldom a good idea to advise a man to get in touch with his feelings, because the only feeling most men have besides self-pity is rage. When men get in touch with their feelings they tend to put their fists through Sheetrock and other expensive forms of expression. Male rage is an emotional black hole, an imploded sun with gravity so intense that not even emotions can escape. Unlike a black hole in space, which is a supernova that implodes into nothingness, a psychic black hole is invisible until it explodes into an all-consuming fire. Scientists have found that when they stimulate this portion of the brain in experimental subjects, the men develop uncontrollable urges to go to demolition derbies and monster-truck rallies. Twenty-four hours after this experiment most subjects still believed that pickup trucks could fly as they do in TV ads. An amazing seventy-two hours later, the men were exposed to army recruitment brochures and all volunteered for unspecified commando raids.

Self-Pity

Self-pity and rage are the two sides of the same manic-depressive coin for most men. Together they take up an awesome portion of male neurology, leaving less available computing power for more immediate and important tasks. The so-called "Look-what-you-made-me-do" lobe is responsible for the latent bully in so many men. This isn't the clumsy bullying of our school days. It's the subtler bullying that blames women for their own victimization, manufactures scapegoats and creates the impression that men are being tyrannized by those whom they tyrannize.

Competitiveness

Men are very competitive about things that don't matter, which is what makes them such terrible drivers. Combined with rage, competitiveness makes men crazy when someone passes them on the freeway, even though they're already going over the speed limit. On the other hand, competitiveness combined with self-pity makes men strut and pout when women beat them at tennis. Male competitiveness probably springs from some ancient, prehuman display behavior, like that of the jackdaw who steals bits of ribbon and shiny objects to furnish his nest so as to attract a jackdawette. This means that competitiveness is one of the lower brain-stem functions we share with birds. One can only wonder why we didn't hold onto something more useful as we evolved, such as the ability to instinctively navigate our way home in lousy weather.

Regrets

Men can be divided into three groups: 1) those who regret what they did in their youth; 2) those who regret what they didn't do; and 3) those who have absolutely no recollection of the whole period. These men probably should have regrets for whatever they most likely did. All three are safe for women to be around. The first is too worn out to be a nuisance, the second is still too timid and the third is befuddled to this day. Like most highfalutin sentiments, regrets are nothing but the sound of a tree falling in an uninhabited forest.

Testosterone Toys: Power Tools, Stupid Sports Statistics, W.C. Fields and Three Stooges film festivals.

The difference between men and boys isn't the price of their toys but the decibel level of those toys. Little boys have to make "vroom-vroom" sounds when they play on their tricycles; big boys take the mufflers off their Harleys. Our grandfathers built their houses with nothing but a hammer and a hand saw. Now every craft project requires power tools that break noise-abatement ordinances. Ever wonder where ideas like that come from? They're lodged right here, in an overactive portion of the brain stem, one of the oldest and least developed portions of the brain – the part that we share with other primates, most mammals and some of the more clever reptiles. That means that as soon as the first proto-humans crawled out of the caves, the males were going "woo-woo-woo" and poking each other in the eyes.

Sweaty Sex

Men have always used sports metaphors for sex, a trait that irritates women, particularly those who view romance more as an aesthetic than an athletic experience. Men used to talk about "scoring," about "getting to first, second or third base," of "hitting" on women" or even "home runs." Most of their male friends realized they were just telling fish stories because the subtext was always about the one that got away. But society changes, sports change and even men (however slowly) change. We still think of sex as the world's most wonderful game, but our frame of reference is different. We realize that sex, like video games, offers an exhilarating variety of buttons to play with. As in tennis, where the racquet's sweet spot is so important, we spend thrilling, if frustrating, hours searching for the G-spot. Sex, we have learned from our women, is a game of handball, and everyone knows that a serious athlete needs a personal trainer. Cable TV offers a wide variety of both sporting events and sexual encounters for the couch spuds. Most important, protective equipment has become mandatory to prevent injury and save lives. Many men are beginning to prefer sex to sports because you have to give up sports when your knees give out.

Mixed Marriages: Was Grandma Right?

*M*ixed marriages *do* work. You just have to make some little adjustments, like moving across the continent, changing your name and entering the government's witness-protection plan.

America has indeed returned to tradition in the last decade. Unfortunately, one of our oldest traditions is a certain religious tension. Catholics and Lutherans get tense around each other – so do Baptists and Episcopalians – and a fundamentalist (Christian or Islamic) can make an entire family reunion go rigid with religious tension by announcing an upcoming marriage to a Jew.

But the major religious tensions are external to the happy couple, who have obviously overcome their theological qualms about falling in love with each other. It's the relatives who make the fuss that goes down in history – Papa Capulet and Papa Montague, Mama Hatfield and Mama McCoy and so on.

Families forget that in today's world they are extraneous. We no longer live in quaint Thuringian villages where disobedient children were thrown into abandoned Melmac quarries. Nowadays, a family that gets in the way of someone's happiness and/or sanity gets cut afloat faster than you can say, "You'll do it my way or not at all!"

We're left with the divisions that really matter to the bride and groom themselves. Trying to blend two sets of apartment furniture is bad enough. Even harder is trying to mash two different attitudes into the Cuisinart to come up with a happy blend.

If you find yourself in a mixed marriage, as all of us do, here are some truths of which you should be aware. Remember that you're going to live with this person for a long time, so it only makes sense to choose your spouse with as much care as you'd choose a roommate.

1. For many people, "holier-than-thou" has been replaced by "recycles-more-than-thou." Going through the garbage to see if your lazy sweetie threw any aluminum cans or glass jars into the biodegradable waste stream may be correct from an environmental standpoint, but unless you are tactful, you may find your marriage recycled.

2. The worst accidents happen in the dark. Men who habitually leave the seat up on the toilet seldom live to a ripe old married age unless they reform. The difference between the seat and the cold porcelain stool itself is only a couple of inches, but many a bride who expected neither the extra drop nor the cool sensation (particularly if she actually hit water) at 3 A.M. has been moved to fury and a desire to talk about it at length with the malefactor.

3. Mutual orgasms aren't necessary to a happy marriage, but mutual attitudes about morning are. Some people are bright-eyed and bushy-tailed at 7 A.M. while others look like characters out of a Russian novel at that ungodly hour. This is a basic personality difference, and only patience, understanding and megadoses of caffeine will help.

4. Fresh air is a wonderful thing, but some people feel it should stay outside in December, while others want to invite it in. Just remember that most people believe that throwing up the sash in December is justified only if you can actually *see* Saint Nicholas.

5. If you fancy yourself a gourmet cook and you are marrying someone whose idea of pasta is limited to elbow macaroni, you may find yourself simmering, stewing and eventually boiling over.

6. One of the wonders of our electronic age is that we can have life-and-death struggles over things our grandparents never heard about. It's easier to get married and mix *his* kids with *your* kids than it is to mix his compact discs with your vinyl albums.

7. If your idea of a security blanket is a bed sheet tucked in so tight that no bug-eyed monster (or older brother) can grab at your toes, don't be surprised if your more laid-back partner considers tucked sheets painful and verging on bondage.

8. Some people depend on a digital clock to tell them when it's *exactly* 9:53:25. Other folks set their clocks ahead four minutes so they'll never be late, and some characters think that a 9 A.M. appointment means "sometime in the morning." A marriage that tries to blend these notions of time is in for major clock-shock.

9. Separate checking accounts have saved many a marriage. Some people never balance their checkbooks. Some round up the figure so they have surpluses at the end of the month. Some computerize their checkbooks with spreadsheets. But most of us rely on voodoo mathematics and the U.S. mail to bring us notice that our Ready Reserve is about to implode.

10. Are you laptop compatible with your mate? Is the apple of your eye a Mac, while you're an IBM? Does he claim to be a mainframe, when he's really only a clone from Singapore? Better check out your modems before exchanging disks.

Why Are Men Extraneous to Weddings?

*M*en will take more interest in weddings when Black and Decker starts making a line of cordless wedding accessories. Until then, men are about as useless as a bag of fingernail clippings when it comes to weddings.

Weddings are a woman's world. Always have been and probably always will be. That's because men are cynical and women are not. Women see weddings as a way to honor a sister who is mystically joining the great river of life. They want to participate in this joyous celebration. Men see weddings as a way to honor a brother who is having more sex than he'll ever have again for the rest of his life, and they want no part of it. There's nothing like a little jealousy to sour a good party.

Men would rather do something exciting, like detassel corn or balance their checkbooks, than plan a wedding. Their absence from the planning process increases the feminization of weddings, which further excludes them from the process. This is why Martha Stewart got the etiquette contract at K Mart instead of John Madden and why the Wedding Expo isn't held in conjunction with the Boat Show.

Men will get serious about weddings when the Sharper Image opens a wedding registry for grooms.

The Wedding Shower: Party Hats on MBAs

Showers are a fun way to get together with other women and get a little silly. Add a little punch, some dessert, fill in the gaps with presents and you've got a sure-fire good time. But nobody's allowed to get rowdy because some darned fool invited everybody's mother. Why is this? Men never invite the father of the groom to the stag party, and all hell breaks loose. But women invite their mothers, and everybody ends up playing children's games for party favors. This doesn't seem fair.

Showers may have been the first form of networking. Men may get together with "the guys," but women have a data base with the address of every friend, every family member, every colleague and most of their high school and college classmates. This inclusiveness has led some families to establish de facto rules about shower invitations. On the man's side, first cousins and only those aunts and great-aunts not actually confined to a nursing home are invited. On the bride's side, *everyone* is fair game. The same goes for professional colleagues, although some people get real sassy if you invite them to a wedding shower after meeting them only once in the elevator.

Showers are the coronation festivities of the princess bride. At the shower, the bride-to-be is treated with the sort of condescending deference that women give to a hugely pregnant woman. She sits, serene on her bridal throne (which is decorated with balloons or inflated condoms, depending on how many elderly aunts have been invited) and receives expensive presents. In short, she's treated as if she's made of eggshell. The whole process resembles the way some tribes worship a virgin till they throw her into the volcano.

Society has moved on, but showers have not. Showers today have no relationship to any part of your life or times. You might well have an MBA and be a corporate vice president, but when you attend a shower, you'll be playing children's birthday games for party favors.

One hot new trend – theme showers – can pump new vigor into the traditional wedding shower. There are books full of fun themes: a calorie-counter shower, where the guests wear chest banners, as beauty contestants do, reading "Marriage is like dieting – forever!" Or a Las Vegas shower for the bingo crowd. Theme showers reach their sordid peak in what might be called fantasy showers. Before you ask people to act out your fantasies in public, please remember that if your fantasies were of any interest to anybody else, they wouldn't be fantasies.

The best theme shower is the romantic-novel shower, where you can let your imagination run wild as you re-create the setting of your favorite

WEDDING SHOWER GAME LEADS TO NATIONAL MEDIA ATTENTION

When Alycia went to Krys Spelbrink's wedding shower, she hadn't planned to play "Off-the-Top-of-Your-Head," where the ladies have to eat a piece of cake from a paper plate on top of their heads.

And she never dreamed that Krys would send the tape of the shower to *America's Funniest Home Videos*. Now a local celebrity of sorts, Alycia quips, "Thank God it wasn't a lingerie shower!"

"bodice ripper" novel. Set the scene by decorating your home so it resembles a magnolia garden, a Kentucky country estate or a moated chateau with hussars and dragoons and chevaliers. For entertainment, read one of the novel's juicy parts, substituting the couple's names for the characters'. Or have guests act out the scene, videotape it and give it to the couple as a memento. I bet they'll just treasure the heck out of it.

Modern Showers for Today's Bride

We need showers that reflect the interests of today's modern youth rather than those of their aunts and mothers (when was the last time you met a twenty-four-year-old excited about climbing into a poodle skirt for a Nifty Fifties Shower?). Here are a few simple suggestions.

The Voice-Mail Shower

All guests check their appointment books and promise to be at the shower, but then work late, phone their apologies to the bride's voice-mail and have a courier rush the gift over to her house.

The Girls' Weekend Shower

A dozen women cash in their Frequent Flyer coupons to fly to a friend's condo in Florida for a weekend of power lounging by the pool, telling horror stories from work and assuring the bride that getting married is probably her best option.

The "I'm-Just-Waitressing-Till-I-Get-Through-School" Shower

The bride's friends all come to the restaurant, sit in her section and leave a good tip without arguing about who owes what. The maid of honor announces to everybody in the restaurant that the bride is getting married soon, and if she had any money, she wouldn't be taking time away from her studies to pour coffee, so would the rest of you cheapskates cough up a decent tip for a change.

The Sympathy Shower

None of the bride's friends can stand the groom and no one can figure out why she's marrying him. But she's still their friend, so they get together to give her some support and some items she might need, like the name of a good divorce lawyer.

The Résumé Shower

Perfect for someone just starting in the business world or someone with a job in a dysfunctional office. Get the marriage off to a good start with what she really needs: a well-typed, up-to-date résumé and some good interviewing clothes.

The Holistic Shower

Since preparing for a wedding is so stressful, why add to the bride's problems by pumping her full of refined white sugar? Treat the whole person by getting her a good full-body massage, some Kitaro tapes and a crystal or two. Cast her I Ching, read her Tarot and chart her biorhythms.

Searching for the Stag Party: A Snipe Hunt for the Nineties

*E*very woman believes in her heart of hearts that all grooms have wild stag parties filled with disgusting goings-on. Yet when pressed, most brides will hoot when you ask if *their* fiancé had one of those wild parties: "Charlie? *My* Charlie? Don't be ridiculous!"

Men themselves are baffled about stag parties. Put them on the spot and they'll admit that while they *personally* have never gone to one, they may know a friend of a friend who once heard about a friend of his who went to this weird party.

That's the secret to stag parties – it's always some *other* guy who does it. The guys at the factory think it's those socialites because they're used to hosting parties. The yuppies think it's the union guys because blue-collar types are so wild and crazy. Jocks think artists have all the fun because they know nude models, while artsy types think jocks still get all the girls, just as they did in high school. Older grooms think those out-of-control kids are the guilty parties and the guys getting married right out of high school think it's the older, established dudes who can afford stuff like that.

Maybe the name – *stag* party – gives it an unwarranted totemic power. Picture a stag – deep chested, with a huge rack of horns, perched atop a windswept rocky promontory. Does that honestly describe the average guy who's about to get married? Let's call it a badger party instead. A badger is a squat, low-slung critter that scampers around and has some attitude problems in the morning. That sounds more like the guys I know.

So what *do* men do at badger parties? The same thing men in New Guinea do in their male-only *Haus Tamburans* – just hang out. They smoke a little, drink a little more, play some cards and tell dumb jokes. Then they go home early. They drink, but not so much they'll feel like hell tomorrow. Some guys will venture out – as a group – to some exotic dancer place to watch women mud wrestle or even wrestle in Jell-O. They'll hoot and scratch and have some beer and then go home and have boozy nightmares about Jell-O between their toes. Pretty innocent stuff.

Men at bachelor parties say they're mourning the end of bachelorhood, but they all know that once a man gets married, he's got it made. Married men are healthier, happier and live longer than bachelors. Husbands are also happier with marriage than wives are, although statistically women do outlive their husbands. Bachelor parties put on a long face just to keep from gloating.

Guys are pretty health-conscious nowadays. Maybe the true bachelor party for the Nineties would feature an aerobics instructor popping out of a bran muffin. But don't waste any time looking for it.

Wedding Invitations as Disincentives

Wedding guest lists are drawn from two groups: relatives, with whom you share great chunks of genetic information (which is what makes them so irritating) and friends, who know things about you that none of your relatives should ever be allowed to hear.

Up to the day of your wedding, you've kept your relatives from learning what your friends know about you and you've protected your friends from your family. On your wedding day, everybody gets together and tells awful stories about you.

Your relatives look at your friends and sadly think how far you've come down in the world to associate with such people. Your friends look at your relatives and are amazed at how well you've done, coming from such a crowd. (Later, your relatives will recall that they never did think you'd amount to much, and your friends will decide that you haven't come as far as they thought after all.)

This is why people cry at weddings. You might consider seating your friends on one side of the church and both families on the other side, instead of dividing the crowd between the bride's side and the groom's side.

Some clever people have solved this problem by inviting only relatives to the church service and only friends to the reception. To accomplish this without offending people, you must subtly invite people to *dis*invite themselves from the part of the event that would be inappropriate for them. The trick is to use two different engraved invitations.

Send this invitation to your problematic relatives:

Mr. & Mrs. Delmar Quackenbush
invite you to the wedding of their daughter
Lisa Jean Quackenbush
to
Shawn Smith
at House of Good Manners
Episcopal Church.

———

The reception following will feature
painfully loud music
played by androgynous thugs,
indifferent but highly spiced food,
and no booze.

Meanwhile, send this invitation to those friends who would be shocked to find out what your relatives are like.

Mr. & Mrs. Delmar Quackenbush
invite you to a reception
honoring the wedding of their daughter
Lisa Jean Quackenbush
to
Shawn Smith
at House of Good Manners
Episcopal Church.

———

The wedding itself will be really awful, with lots of sexist allusions, a totally incompetent soloist singing dorky songs, and no booze.

Guidelines for Inviting Relatives

1. While you have less leeway here than in selecting friends, remember that any relative who, in an Edgar Allan Poe novel, would have been locked in a secret room, probably doesn't enjoy getting out in public. In other words, don't invite someone if you're afraid to make any sudden moves around him.

2. Although a wedding is clearly a religious occasion, any relative who would bring an annotated Bible to argue with the minister about a scripture verse used in the ceremony will be happier at home with some pamphlets and a TV minister. Let sleeping fanatics lie – far away from you.

3. If champagne is to be served, remember that alcoholism runs in families and in some cases turns into an out-and-out marathon. Relatives commonly described as "colorful" or "flamboyant" might benefit from a chaperone. Then again, you could just have them shipped to detox.

4. Churches are always overheated because many otherwise sweet, grandmotherly types are convinced that if they get cold they will fall down and break a hip. To avoid this, they douse themselves with an industrial-strength perfume solution to warn off oncoming traffic. If you can smell Aunt Gloria before you enter the church, imagine what her pewmates are experiencing.

5. You can mix together just about any religious combination you want, but if you have the sort of relative who wears a fur coat over a jogging suit to the grocery store in Florida, you will need to be sure that no animal-rights activists are invited. "The fur will fly" is no longer just a figure of speech.

Guidelines for Inviting Friends

1. Do not include a woman whose idea of dressing up means putting on a clean tube top. In fact, weddings are not a time for creative dressing of any sort, which leaves out much of the artistic community.

2. Never invite a political friend who might want to save the world, starting at your wedding. Reformers should remember that the only successful mass movement ever started at a wedding was two thousand years ago at a wedding in Cana.

3. Friends who use "Shit Happens" bumper stickers to cover up rust spots on their cars are unlikely to be comfortable at a reception with valet parking. The valets may be even more uncomfortable when these folks hang around them instead of going inside.

4. Weddings are food festivals. Friends who have found their life's work crusading against sugar, carbohydrates, animal products, cholesterol, meat or whatever the craze of the month may be will not be comfortable watching your relatives go back for third servings. You can dissuade them from attending by hinting that you'll be serving only Kentucky Fried Chicken and Twinkies at the reception.

5. If all your or your partner's old college friends are planning a reunion at your wedding, consider not attending. These champagne-fueled reunions often lead to all sorts of revelations, and it may come as a shock to discover how many close, personal friends your spouse spent time sharing and caring with in past years.

Countdown to Bliss: Sleeping in Hand-Lotioned Gloves

*B*ridal magazines love to help brides count down to their weddings because it is such a logical sequence for selling goods. On the other hand, you don't have to be a rocket scientist to realize that countdowns are usually associated with large, explosive items setting off for unknown regions, which may describe some marriages very well indeed.

If you study wedding countdowns you'll learn that there are still some serious differences between what's expected of men and what's demanded of women in today's wedding world. Women have a six-foot list of details to attend to, while the man's only task is to show up at the church at 11:30.

Here's the most honest wedding countdown you'll find anywhere.

One Year Prior

Groom:

🚶 Work hard at job. Get into a good softball league.

Bride:

🚶 Settle on groom. Wonder about it, then decide to go for it anyway.

🚶 Decide what fashion statement you want to make with your wedding gown. Wonder if you could really wear that gown with your waist, shoulders, hips and chest.

🚶 Send a tasteful announcement of your engagement and glossy four-by-five head and shoulders photo to your hometown newspaper. Then send one to his hometown newspaper, so his high school girlfriends can eat their hearts out. You might even want to send announcements to the newspapers in the town or towns where you now live, as well as the town in which you will live after you're married. This is a big step and you deserve congratulations!

🚶 Buy a medium-capacity business computer to handle all your wedding record keeping. You'll need to keep track of press announcements, shower and wedding invitations sent and responses, gifts received, thank-you notes sent, seating charts, vendor appointments, accounts payable and all those little notes to yourself.

🚶 List of all the friends you want in your wedding:

Cross out everybody you're seriously not talking to.

Cross out anybody more than thirty pounds lighter or heavier than you.

Cross out anybody more than four inches taller or shorter than you.

Cross out anybody who won't be a lot of fun to have around.

Cross out anybody whose religious, racial or ethnic background, sexual preferences, disability or nation of origin might upset any of your relatives.

Cross out anybody who would have financial difficulty paying for both a bridesmaid's gown and a nice wedding present.

Nine Months Prior

Groom:

⚦ Get a bunch of James Bond videos and check them out for sexy honeymoon sites.

⚦ Move your clothes, records, CDs and tapes to the bride's apartment, or vice versa. Consider moving the VCR.

⚦ Get HIV tested as a couple. It's the thing to do.

Bride:

⚦ Set the date. Choose a church, preferably one where the minister, priest, rabbi, imam or channeler will at least recognize you by sight.

⚦ Tour the better hotels, country clubs or VFW halls and choose a reception site. Any location that requires a damage deposit three times the rental fee might be used to a rougher crowd, but only you know your friends.

⚦ Buy a memory album. Sit up nights writing everything that pops into your head, till you can't stand it.

⚦ Choose a maid of honor. Use same criteria as in selecting the wedding party, only more so. Meet with her to plan your first big shower.

⚦ Establish your wedding budget and ask both families for contributions.

⚦ Have your first really big fight with your mother about your wedding when she suggests that "contributions" means "shakedown."

⚦ Try to discuss the wedding for more than fifteen minutes with your fiancé. Instead, get into your first big fight with your fiancé about the wedding. Write about it in your memory album. Wonder later whether to tear the page out.

Six Months Prior

Groom:

⚦ Find a place to live and scrape together the damage deposit. Move everything again.

Bride:

⚦ Take control of your life and appearance! Start a serious program of beauty care that will cover everything, from toe to tippy-top.

⚦ If you have your professional color analysis done now, you can use it to select the colors of the bridesmaids' gowns, the invitations, the wedding flowers, the limousine, the centerpieces, the reception table linens and the napkins. It's *your* special day and *everything* should complement *you*!

⚦ Spend some time experimenting with your cheekbones! The technology of personalized beauty-care products has changed so much recently, you will be just *amazed* to see what new products are available! Learn how the new personalized beauty-care products can help you make a statement with your face!

🚶 Get serious about your eyes, your best beauty asset! Create captivating colors for *your* eyes for beautiful, eye-catching looks, because everyone knows that beautiful is better!

🚶 Start a good skin-care routine today! There's no better time to start taking good care of your skin and no better gift you can give yourself and your husband!

🚶 Start some serious dieting and hustle your buns down to the club for a personalized exercise program. Water pills two weeks before the wedding won't do the trick!

🚶 Interview wedding photographers. Decide on impulse to give your fiancé a bridal boudoir album as a wedding gift. Panic. Cancel. Reschedule. Get cold feet. Reschedule.

🚶 Offer to help your mother, your future mother-in-law and your grandmothers pick out their gowns in colors that complement your professional color analysis. Stay cheerful even if they tell you to shove it.

🚶 Select a theme for your reception (just like a prom!) and interview professional musicians who can perform the kind of music that complements your theme. Debate whether to use live musicians or a disco service at your reception. Sign a contract with one and wish you'd gone with the other.

🚶 Get into a screaming fit with your mother about the wedding plans. When that doesn't work, try logic. Then just leave the house.

Three Months Prior

Groom:

🚶 Review your career objectives and get a raise.

🚶 Panic about the honeymoon and buy tickets to anywhere within three time zones.

🚶 Change your insurance and will to name your fiancée as beneficiary. Suddenly it's all very real.

Bride:

🚶 Order all your special decorations for the reception: engraved napkins and swizzle-sticks; four-by-five-foot color display photograph of you and your fiancé to exhibit behind wedding cake; balloons that spell out "Congratulations, Peaches and Fred," or any other little item that catches your fancy.

🚶 Arrange a meeting with your floral design expert to personally design your perfect bouquet, the bridesmaids' arrangements, the boutonnieres and the pretty floral displays for the reception.

🕇 Arrange a meeting with your mother and future mother-in-law at the main post office to pick out a pretty picture stamp for your wedding invitations and response cards.

🕇 Engage a respected calligrapher to address your wedding invitations and announcements. Be sure to include your return address in the front of your wedding invitation or any invitations with wrong address will end up in the Dead Gimme-Letter Office.

🕇 Hold a shower rehearsal with your maid of honor. Put all your living room chairs in a circle and, as your maid of honor hands you random items, practice saying "It's so *cute!*" or "I know just where *this* will go in my new house!" Continue until onset of nausea.

🕇 Schedule a consultation with your wedding-cake stylist. Come away with a two-day sugar buzz after tasting samples. Review any contract signed under such influence.

🕇 Stop arguing with your mother and turn your entire wedding over to her.

Two Months Prior
Groom:

🕇 Consolidate checking accounts, shift all utilities, phone and service bills. Check on credit cards.

🕇 Finish paying for the rings.

Bride:

🕇 Get a new haircut that takes your wedding headpiece into account. Confirm your appointment with the hairdresser to do your hair on your wedding day, requesting that he or she travel to your home to save you time and energy. Engage a top manicurist for the same morning.

🕇 As they arrive, record each wedding present on the computer, thoroughly describing each gift item, giving place of purchase and price. Call store if you're uncertain about the retail price. Use the computer to make up a little chart of comparative gift prices. Print out an appropriate thank-you note immediately.

🕇 Review your homeowner's insurance to assure that your wedding gifts are adequately covered. If not, jack up the policy to match the flow of goodies.

🕇 Interview makeup artists and experiment with new makeup styles that perfectly blend your personality with what the wedding dress is trying to say. Try not to giggle when you say this.

🕇 Get serious about your nail-care routine.

Six Weeks Prior

Groom:

- Ask a bunch of the guys on your softball team if they'd mind being in your wedding.
- Check the invitation list and make sure that no old girlfriends are included.

Bride:

- Get rid of the rough skin on your knees and elbows with pumice stone if necessary. Sleep wearing lotion-saturated gloves and socks to help soften your feet and hands.
- Don't let your perfect wedding reception be ruined because your groom, your father or your future father-in-law aren't tip-top dancers! Don't be afraid to enlist professional help by enrolling them in a reputable dance studio.

One Month Prior

Groom:

- Find some tuxedos that all the guys will agree to wear.

Bride:

- Discuss rehearsal dinner with groom and get firm commitment that he *will* attend.
- Plan lodging for any out-of-town guests, relatives, ushers and bridesmaids. Make sure nobody is sleeping with the wrong person, as far as you can help.
- Keep writing those thank-you notes for early gift arrivals. Promptness counts!

Two Weeks Prior

Groom:

- Check out super-stretch limousines. See if there's still any money in the budget for them.

Bride:

- Start sleeping in a body stocking saturated with a gentle, scented lotion to give you that special, soft "southern belle" skin all over.
- Attend the fourth and final wedding shower (the famous Senile Female Relatives and Their Distant Co-workers Shakedown). Please remember that these women lead precariously balanced lives and it would only upset them to hear the details of what it means to practice safe sex in the nineties.

One Week Prior

Groom:

- Attend groom's party. Leave when some dork brings out an XXX-rated video called "Body Parts on Parade."

Bride:

- Stock up on extra hosiery for the wedding and your honeymoon. Your attendants would surely appreciate the gift of some fine hosiery.
- Sneak upstairs and try on your wedding gown to make sure it still fits after all those cake and ice cream showers.
- Try on your headpiece after your new hairdo. Try not to cry. Look for the "Dear Abby" article about how a woman was able to sue her hairdresser for a bad job.

🕴 Send wedding announcements and five-by-seven-inch glossy photos to the five newspapers to which you sent engagement announcements. Even if you live in a town so small that everybody already knows you're getting married and why, it's nice to have the attention. Arrange these announcements in your scrapbook.

🕴 Treat all your attendants to a consultation with a professional eyebrow cosmetologist. Don't tweeze, wax or pluck too close to your special day – you've got to give the irritation time to subside. Make sure that none of your bridesmaids' eyebrows are too bushy, too sparse or otherwise unsightly. You wouldn't want your special day ruined by less-than-perfect eyebrows on everybody.

🕴 Make up the seating chart for the reception dinner, taking into account relatives who won't talk to each other. For example, don't seat someone from MADD next to the family lush, and try to keep your NRA uncle as far as possible from your animal-rights friends.

🕴 Beg your fiancé to demand that all his idiot friends actually show up on the wedding day to serve as ushers.

One Day Prior

Groom:

🕴 Don't party too hearty. You wouldn't want a hangover to rob you of your wedding memories!

🕴 Make sure the best man has both the ring and the clergyman's fee. Take appropriate action if he does not.

Bride:

🕴 Put a wad of Kleenex in the sleeve of your gown. You don't want to have to worry about your nose running during the ceremony!

🕴 Plan some special way to say thank you to your parents on the morning of your wedding. Don't just assume that your leaving home will be reward enough.

🕴 Relax and pamper yourself with a bubble bath. Try not to get obsessive about the wedding. Settle for not drowning yourself in the bathtub.

🕴 *Don't* overeat and blimp up! *Don't* eat tomatoes or your shoulders will break out with zits! *Don't* eat any peanuts or you'll get gas! *Don't* eat chocolate or your face will break out! *Don't* eat anything that will give you terrible breath! *Don't* have more than a half-glass of wine or you'll get bags under your eyes! *Don't* eat carrots or you'll get excess ear wax! *Do* eat a little something or you'll probably faint during the ceremony. *Don't* worry yourself to tatters! *Do* maintain your special sense of humor and have a *special* day!

BRIDAL RACE HEATS UP

The qualifying heats were run today in the Beauty Trap Bridal Open, where women compete against other women for prize weddings instead of competing against men for careers.

Events run today included the First-Marriage-After-School Sprints; the Biggest-Wedding Mile, the Longest-Reception Marathon, the Fifty-Day-Diet Dash and the Hubby Toss.

Said race organizer G. Harold Farnswell: "The Open actually makes girls better wives by getting all that competitiveness out of their systems."

The Marital-Industrial Complex

*I*t may be nothing but historical coincidence, but as weddings have grown in size and spectacle, circuses have faded from our cultural life.

Maybe that's because weddings are a better marketing tool than circuses. Circuses used to parade tigers and elephants through small towns for the amazement of the yokels. Then, the local businesses hoped, the yokels would hang around and spend some money. Today, if everything an average young couple bought or was given when they got married was put on wagons, it would make a longer and costlier parade than those old circuses could ever muster.

American enterprise is in love with weddings not because business people are a bunch of raging romantics, but because weddings employ caterers, jewelers, beauticians, florists, photographers, consultants and seamstresses. Young married couples rent country clubs, hotels, limousines, VFW halls and honeymoon cabins, on which they or their parents pay 18.5 percent annual interest on their maxed-out credit cards.

Newlyweds go on a once-in-a-lifetime buying binge, acquiring washers and dryers, apartments, furniture, china, microwaves, clothing, stoves, towels, refrigerators, silverware and flatware, bedding, crystal, automobiles and gewgaws of all description. We're not just talking about a little work for free-lance videographers. We're talking about playing house with real money. We're talking Durable Goods! That's one of the Major Economic Indicators that the President of the United States and the dude who runs the Federal Reserve Board sit up nights worrying about.

If we want America to get back on track as a major economic power, we've got to convert our military-industrial complex into a wedding mall. When the people who specialize in $850 toilet seats find out where the *big* money is, they'll beat their swords into bridal accessories.

The Nuptial Trade Fair

*B*ridal shows should be festive affairs, full of laughing young women and their approving mothers. In reality, they are a grim business crammed with hordes of desperate women of all ages reminding one of the survivors of a terrible earthquake waiting for the Red Cross to arrive.

Everything a bride has come to suspect and fear about weddings is proved true at a bridal show. *"Your* wedding?" Don't be silly! Weddings belong to the Marital-Industrial Complex, but you can get a short-term lease on one. For the M-I Complex, personalizing your wedding means hot-stamping your names on napkins, not doing something that might cut into the cash flow.

A hundred years ago, when weddings were primarily religious celebrations, not simply events staged at churches, a bridal show would have seemed like an invasion of the temple by money-changers. But times, expectations and desperation levels change. Today's bride works full-time. Her mother probably works part-time, if not full-time. Men are no more helpful than they've ever been. *Somehow* the bride's got to find the vendors to provide all the pieces of her fantasy wedding.

At bridal shows, corporate caterers give away free cake from their booth right next to the medically supervised rapid-weight-loss program.

automatic calligraphy machine attracts the men, who feel more comfortable with its technology than they do with the florist who gushes about the emotions flowers evoke. The biggest crowds gather at the nail-care booth, where women line up to get a quickie manicure and personalized nail-care tips.

Mannequins are passé – now wedding gowns and tuxes are displayed on automatons at bridal shows. A clever sales technique is to feature both automatons and live models behaving like automatons – you're supposed to guess which is which. It isn't hard: Real people don't have industrial-strength power cords running up their skirts.

Wedding gowns are the big-ticket items that drive this economy, and the fashion show is the evening's highlight. It's usually the typical New York/Old South stuff: The male models swagger and grind their hips. The women hide behind parasols and flirt.

Nowadays, wrapping yourself and your business interests in the flag is popular, so you'll find themes like "A Patriotic Celebration." The male models carry big flags as they run up and down the runway and the women dress in red, white or blue gowns. Sort of implies that it's downright treasonable to spend less than $20,000 on your wedding.

The emcee is full of ideas for the bride who wants to spend a lot of money quickly. Like treating her entire family by taking them on the honeymoon cruise. Or exercising "Your Choice for Fashion Perfection" by insisting that every male at the wedding – not just the wedding party, but the grandfathers, the guys from the hockey team and casual work associates – all come attired in black tie and tux.

And of course, there's music – like the song I call the "Gimme!" song: "If I can't have my kind of wedding, / I don't want to get married at all, / If it's not a big wedding, / I won't get married at all!" Or the "Obey" song: "I'm an old-fashioned girl and I'd just love to obey someone."

Maybe that stuff plays well in southern belle country, but it's more likely that these ideas come from the distant youth of the men who organize these events.

I don't know how many gowns they sell at those shows, but I suppose everybody doesn't go away too irritated to spend money. Brides develop a pretty thick skin on the way to their wedding reception. They need it.

The Ultimate How-to Magazine

*B*ridal magazines are the original home shopping network – a thousand pages of advertising per month, with just enough editorial content to qualify for certain postal rates. They're filled with articles written in the breathless style of a high school cheerleader on a caffeine jag. The titles are provocative, but the answers aren't: "Why are men and women so different?" The answer: "Well, they just are."

Putting on a wedding is a complex enterprise, and bridal magazines are there to help with advice about etiquette. In an age when dining out means not using the drive-through window at McDonald's, modern couples need help resolving moral dilemmas, such as what to do if a bridesmaid's eyebrows grow together and she refuses to tweeze them.

Editorial changes come slowly to bridal magazines, which lag slightly behind society as a whole and well behind what's current with young people. That's because during the eighteen months the average subscriber reads the magazine while she prepares for her wedding, her mother is reading it too. And while Momma is indignant that the magazine is full of all this birth-control talk putting ideas in young people's heads, her daughter is more interested in hearing what the experts have to say about a little light bondage.

We all read magazines that tell us how to deal with and manipulate our world. Men – when they read at all – read about how to manipulate power tools or inanimate objects. A typical boy article would be "How to Turn Victorian Staircase Banisters on a Home Lathe." Women are less interested in testosterone toys than in relationships, so women's magazines are jam-packed with ways to manipulate other people (particularly those mysterious men) for one's own benefit. "10 Ways to Tone Up Your Thighs to *MAKE* Him Propose!" for example.

Nowadays, bridal magazines, not ancient ethnic customs, are the arbiters of wedding traditions. That's not necessarily bad. There were reasons we left those old traditions behind. For one thing, the ancients weren't exactly crazy about women, and for another, traditions are messy. A typical ancient tradition would require the village women to smear the naked bride with yam pulp to purify her and crank her fertility up to the point where she practically became a baby factory. You don't have to be too alert to figure out that most young women don't think like that nowadays. So in place of genuine traditions, we do stuff like sing "Sunrise, Sunset" at Jewish weddings or serve Swedish meatballs at, well, just about everybody's wedding.

With the influence of the national bridal magazines, even regional differences in wedding customs have given way to economic distinctions. If every bride from Shin Pond, Maine, to Kauakaiakaola Heiau, Hawaii, can see and lust after the same dress, then the distinction will be made in terms of which woman can afford which dress. Regional and ethnic distinctions have melted into a nationwide system of class distinctions, unspoken and secret, right out there on the church steps.

If there is a downside to the bridal magazines, it is their message that no compromises need to be made, that a bride can have everything she wants to make her wedding Perfect, or Flawless, or a Once-in-a-Lifetime Extravaganza.

Fairy-tale weddings – where a princess can do whatever she wants despite the financial consequences and can order people around on her whim, and where the groom is a passive, uninvolved observer – are a terrible model for real-life marriage.

Maybe someday we'll think of weddings as a time for sensible shoes and wedding magazines will publish articles about honeymoon hotels in Minot, North Dakota. Maybe, but don't cancel your subscription just yet.

Bad Ideas for Your Wedding

"It's *my* wedding, so I should be able to do whatever I want."
It's surprising how often you run into this phrase given as an excuse to bust the budget. It should be a true-false question on a test given to see if someone's mature enough to get married. Say "True," and you're back to the sandbox.

"This is a once-in-a-lifetime experience."
Relax and take a look at the divorce statistics. Unless you spend more time establishing a relationship than you did ordering the flowers, you'll be back. Recidivists are now treated to extravagant second, third and even fourth "encore" weddings. But as any actor knows, the applause dies quickly when you take too many curtain calls.

"My wedding has to be *perfect*."
Nothing in this world is perfect except the deity, who refuses to have anything to do with the organizational details of a wedding. In the world of glossy advertising, *perfect* means *expensive*. A *perfect* diamond, the *perfect* dress, the *perfect* reception, means more money than you can afford. This is Donald Trump-type thinking, and no one particularly wants to end up like that anymore. Odd how no one ever talks about a *perfect* spouse. Perhaps even the most idealistic people realize the need to compromise somewhere.

"I have to do everything myself or it won't get done."
Generations of South American generals have used this excuse to usurp other people's power. Don't start out by treating your groom as if he were a banana republic. Perhaps the groom wouldn't have thrown a fit when the store didn't supply the exact shade of pink candles you wanted. Preparing for a marriage, as in all of life, the question is not whether something is done *perfectly*, but whether it needs to be done at all.

Getting Married in Someone Else's Pants (and a Clip-on Tie)

Most American men wear tuxedos only twice in their lives – at their senior prom and at their wedding. Proms are a lot like weddings, although you're more likely to double-date on prom night.

Lots of men own their own tuxedos, and they're just ordinary guys – like piano-bar pianists, maître d's, symphony flautists, members of men's glee clubs and certain wedding photographers. The purchase cost of a tuxedo is equal to only two or three rentals, so if you plan to be married again before you gain a lot of weight, you might be ahead of the game to buy.

Most grooms rent tuxedos as a kind of fashion insurance against looking like a total moron in twenty years when their kids find their wedding pictures. The alternative is to use your wedding to make a "fashion statement." Fashion statements of the past have included Nehru jackets and white three-piece (poly-blend) disco suits. Unfortunately, tuxedos are also a "fashion statement" that changes with the times, which means that in twenty years you will still have to explain to your children why you paid good money to rent such doofy-looking clothes.

Proper formal wear is black or grey. If (and only if) you are in the tropics, white is acceptable. Colors that resemble sherbets or anything made of a metallic lamé are suitable only for Las Vegas lounge performers.

A tuxedo ought to fit properly. The first time you try it on, stand with your back to a mirror and kneel down. That's the view the entire congregation will have of you. You don't want to have your tux bunched up on your butt or shoulders during this solemn moment when your friends are taking pictures of you.

Time of day dictates which formal wear is appropriate. Morning attire is appropriate for a morning wedding, although not for a wedding in mourning. For an afternoon wedding, a grey stroller with a four-in-hand tie and homburg would be nice, but then, knowing how to tie a four-in-hand (where the ends vertically overlap in front) would be nice too.

Tuxedos and dinner jackets are worn for early-evening weddings (5 to 7 P.M.). After-dinner jackets or tie and tails with tasteful white "Phantom of the Opera" half-mask are appropriate for weddings up till 10 P.M. Weddings held after 10 P.M. are generally informal affairs conducted in seedy motels, where the groom wears tiger-print bikini shorts and is conscious during large parts of the ceremony

The Marital-Industrial complex thinks it's perfectly normal for the bride "to put her foot down on the subject of formal attire," or "exercise her choice for fashion perfection." I guess that means throwing a major tantrum unless the groom learns the difference between a shawl collar and a notched lapel real fast.

A Guide to Basic Formal Wear

Morning attire, with its ascot tie and striped trousers, is certain to make your wedding look like a touring production of *My Fair Lady*. This is the proper wear for a morning wedding, but not one that's held so early that your guests will attend in fuzzy pink slippers and Ninja Turtle jammies.

Double-breasted tuxedos come in one- and two-button models, just so you have a wide range of options. Wearing one would be a nice gesture if you are marrying into a major crime family.

A mess jacket, the very trendiest formal wear, is a fitted jacket that stops at the waist. Busboys at banquets wear them. They're particularly nice if you want to show off the groom's tight little buns.

Black full dress is the formal tailcoat with a white wing collar, a piqué formal shirt with a white piqué vest. If you don't know what piqué is, dressing like this would just be ostentatious.

DEAR AUNT MAE, WE'LL ALWAYS TREASURE...

Some wedding presents have great sentimental value. Some have great monetary value. And some just tell you which friends have such bad taste that you need to keep an eye on them at all times. That's valuable too.

You can't protect yourself from presents like this. Everybody gets at least one "Whatzis" at their wedding, usually from a guest who brings it to the church and insists that you open it right there so everybody can see.

You will never be able to get rid of it because that person will want to see it every time he or she comes to your place. Worse, you can't dump it at a garage sale and Goodwill doesn't want it. So just relax and admit that weddings are a kitsch magnet and do what every other married couple has done – grin and hide it.

Taking It at Lace Value: Cloning Cinderella's Gown

No man can distinguish between two wedding dresses. It's like color blindness: Men just don't have the nerve endings in their eyeballs to see that one dress has lace but no beading, while the other dress is solid beading without a stitch of lace. If it's white and it hits the floor, it's a wedding dress to a man.

On the other hand, men can go on for hours about cars as if there was actually a difference between two models.

Wedding gowns and American cars are alike in other ways. Both are overly ornamented and overpriced. Both become rapidly obsolete but are nevertheless the objects of intense sentimentality. Neither is merely a product; both are the attainment of a dream.

But hang it all, they're interchangeable! A wedding gown looks like nothing else in the world, which means that it looks like every other wedding gown. Nuns don't even look like nuns anymore, but you can spot a wedding gown from a weather satellite. I'm surprised that it doesn't show up on Doppler radar in June: "A high-pressure ridge of brides is working its way down the Eastern Seaboard, preceded by kitchen showers, and will be followed by baby squalls pretty soon."

The Big White Dress is a pretty recent invention, dating back only to the 1950s for most of us.

Nobody but the rich could afford a gown that was to be used only once. Most brides just bought the nicest dress they could afford with the intention of wearing it often after the wedding.

I have a theory that what changed all that was the Walt Disney animated movie *Cinderella*, which came out in the 1950s, during the cult of the domestic goddess. *Cinderella* was so romantic and beautiful that impressionable young minds fixated on her beautiful Big White Dress and decided that they had to have one themselves.

Then again, maybe we Americans were just aping Princess Elizabeth's wedding dress the way we aped Princess Di's three decades later. We love copying royalty's wedding dresses, whether real or fictional (and who *wouldn't* want to get married like Julie Andrews in *Sound of Music*?). The great fashion designers have all taken a crack at designing wedding gowns, although the results do seem uncertain. Yves Saint Laurent once designed one called "Baba Russe." The gown was a cocoon, mummifying the bride till only her face and feet showed. She looked like either one of the Russian *Matroyshka* nesting dolls, or a six-foot, lace-covered vibrator. It does seem odd that the bride's arms were functionally bound to her sides by the dress and that only her face showed, but I suppose that's how some men prefer their women.

SOMETHING BORROWED, SOMETHING GREEN...
Brides are discovering that it's no longer enough to have a perfect
wedding. Nowadays, the most admired weddings are also perfectly
biodegradable!

Show your concern for ecology with a designer gown made entirely from
recyclable materials! The fully gathered bell-shaped skirt features a
cathedral train made of shimmering lawn bags. The fitted bubble-wrap,
drop-V bodice is graced by a neckline delicately edged in pop tops and
topped with a patterned six-pack ring lace set off by tiny faux diamonds.
The shoulders are enhanced by pearl detailing. As the crowning glory, the
headpiece is a darling low-density polyethylene rosette with a double
pearl swag.

Pastors, Priests and Rabbis

*R*eligion is like music. We all have a knack for it but only a few of us are good enough to make a living at it. Please keep that *living* part in mind, and don't think you can get away with paying the minister, priest or rabbi less than you would tip the assistant caterer.

Eighty-eight percent of brides get married in a church or synagogue, and it's assumed that the statistics are similar for grooms. Receptions used to be held in church basements, but most church basements have been converted into day-care centers and/or food shelves. Even if they weren't, you can't serve alcohol in a church. The result is that only thirteen percent of wedding receptions nowadays are held in a church or synagogue.

Here are some things you ought to keep in mind when dealing with the clergy, particularly if the last time you saw them was during confirmation or your bar/bas mitzvah.

1. The clergy is not a public utility and therefore cannot be called on in the middle of the night for a spontaneous wedding. In fact, at 3 A.M. many members of the clergy would rather the romantically impatient just sinned now and got married after breakfast, instead of waking them up to insist on proper protocol.

2. Don't even *think* about getting married in some quaint and picturesque little church unless you are a member. Ministers know when they've got a quaint and picturesque little church because lots of strangers (who may or may not be a member of *any* church) call up on short notice wanting to get married there.

3. On the other hand, some quaint and picturesque little churches have begun to capitalize on their quaintness and rent their sanctuaries for all manner of weddings. Some of them derive so much of the parish income from this activity that they barely have time left to schedule their own worship services.

4. If you are overcome with the desire for an unusual wedding, go to Las Vegas, where you can get married at any time or under any circumstances and the entire premarital counseling session consists of "Got the money? Got a ring? Got a bride? You feeling OK? Hello? Hello?"

5. The clergy has problems of its own. A rabbi in Fort Lauderdale was sued because he showed up ninety minutes late to marry two lawyers. The bride and groom contended in their lawsuits that the rabbi's delay caused the guests to run up a bar bill, caused the groom's back condition to flare up and caused the guests to gossip that perhaps the marriage was in trouble. The happy couple sued for seven times the cost of their wedding.

What's Long and Vulgar and Rents by the Hour?

A limousine is not just a very long, vulgar taxicab with pink champagne stains on the crushed velveteen seat covers, where high school students drink and make out on prom night. It's an American symbol of affluence and elegance – swankiness, even – that can be hired by the hour.

That makes it a natural for American weddings.

Limousines have even fancier stuff in them than a customized van. There are cellular phones, little refrigerators, and TVs with VCRs. Many a bride has found her romantic ride from the church interrupted when the groom discovered a baseball game on the tube.

In *The Encyclopedia of Bad Taste*, Michael and Jane Stern report on the stretch-limo war that started in 1982. The first shot was fired by Ultra Limousine Company, which built a thirty-two-foot limo as a promotional gimmick. That was topped by another fellow who first built a fifty-foot limo, then topped his own personal best with a sixty-foot, sixteen-wheel customized Cadillac, complete with a slot machine, putting green, water bed and room for fifty passengers.

But Ultra reasserted itself, building a 104-foot limo with eight TV sets, a ceramic-tiled swimming pool with diving board and a complete kitchen. Ultra also manufactures a hot tub that can be bolted into the trunk of any limo, although the only limo company in Las Vegas that featured hot-tub limos recently went out of business.

We'll know the limo wars are over when we see newlyweds go through the drive-thru lane at White Castle in their own cars.

The Bridesmaid's Tale

There is a conspiracy afoot aimed at unsuspecting young women. The dastardly plan is to make them look odd, out of place and faintly ridiculous. It is known as Operation Bridesmaid.

The basic plot is to choose several young women with total disregard for body type, weight, height and coloring. Then dress these women identically and force them out in front of a large crowd. Make them walk slowly so everyone can get a good look and decide who has the biggest hips or the smallest chest. An Orwellian nightmare? No! It's real and it happens 1.4 million times a year!

Who's behind this conspiracy to humiliate young women? Brides, that's who! This conspiracy is called a wedding, and a wedding is the bride's day to shine. It's her day to be lovelier than she ever has been and ever will be again. How does she do this, considering, on average, that her friends are as good or better looking than she is? She asks them to be bridesmaids!

What better way to stand out than to surround yourself with friends dressed in unflattering clothes, while you wear a dazzling, custom-made gown? Everybody wants to look good, but we'll settle for looking good by comparison. Here are ten warning signs of this conspiracy:

Signs of the Bridal Conspiracy
1. Bows on the butts of large bridesmaids.
2. Low-cut gowns worn by small-chested bridesmaids.
3. Halter-top gowns that gap on large-chested bridesmaids.
4. Colors that flatter no living woman's skin tones.
5. Big, poufy sleeves on broad-shouldered bridesmaids.
6. High-necked dresses on short-necked bridesmaids.
7. Hoop skirts on short bridesmaids.
8. Overly-tight sheath dresses, particularly if they cling.
9. Tea-length dresses on bridesmaids with big ankles.
10. Open-backed gowns on bridesmaids with acne or suntan lines.

Weddings as Photographic Folk Art

*W*edding photography could be considered an American folk art, but then so could landscape paintings on the sides of vans and satellite disks. It's a totally democratic art form, like network TV, and it gets about as much respect.

Wedding photographers are the only professional photographers who don't sell photographs. A wedding photographer is in the business of selling "a part of himself," presumably one of the parts he can safely live without. What he's really selling is his *interpretation* of your wedding, in case you hadn't been paying attention and missed the whole thing.

Wedding photographers are trained to bubble over with enthusiasm about each and every wedding. "Wow!" they gush happily to anyone within earshot, "This is something New and Exciting! I've got some fresh ideas to make it even more special!"

But seriously, folks – burnout is a big problem for wedding photographers. How often could *you* walk backward down the aisle photographing two insanely grinning strangers? Let's be realistic. Weddings are like snowflakes: Each one is unique, but you can go blind trying to find the differences.

New and Alarming Trends in Wedding Photography
The Love Story Slide Show
A wedding is a rite of passage in which two young people enter full adult status, so it seems fitting to remind them that it hasn't been all that long since they were drooling, diapered babies. Some photographers conspire with the parents to gather childhood photos of the bride and groom for a slide show at the reception. If you thought it was embarrassing when your mom showed your high school friends your baby pictures, think how much fun you'll have when everybody at your wedding gets to see snapshots of you on your porta-potty.

Video Interviews of Relatives
Wedding Video sounds hot and fast – MTV goes to church. But your Uncle Herb can't dance as well as Michael Jackson, so instead of jump-cuts, you get interviews with Aunt Ruth reminiscing about all the people you dated, Aunt Ethel complimenting the caterer and your friend Tom doing stupid double entendres.

It's hard to tell what it will be like to watch your wedding video in twenty years. At best, it will be like viewing a rare and wonderful newsreel of a forgotten time. At worst, it could be like watching endless Donna Reed shows in rerun hell.

Pain by Numbers: Paying for the Big Bash

Bridal Boudoir Photography

Bridal boudoir photography is big on the West Coast, where people have apparently channeled their brains into a parallel universe and then left them. Photographers complain that it's not big in the Midwest and the Northeast because of the weather. The absolute ultimate in bridal boudoir photography is the four-by-four-foot photo of the bride, naked as a jay-bird, hanging over the marital bed. You can do that in California because the weather's nice and nobody freezes (and frankly, nobody cares). But up north and back east, guests come to parties all bundled up. Where do they throw their overcoats? On the bed! How can you send your guests into your bedroom if there's a sixteen-square-foot photograph of you in a neon nightie hanging there? It's probably one of the reasons for the continuing migration to the Sun Belt.

Americans believe that you shouldn't have to file for Chapter 11 just to pay for your wedding. Other than that, there are no fiscal guidelines. It's not the wedding itself that's expensive – the minister usually gets less than $100 – but those $3,000 gowns and $25,000 rings do add up. To say nothing of the big reception bash with pink-flamingo ice sculptures, Eiffel Tower cakes made out of white chocolate, or flying a hairdresser in from New York, a make-up artist from Los Angeles and a nail-care professional from Dallas.

And those special little touches! Like renting a pink, super-super-stretch limo with a hot tub in the back. Or covering the entire walls and ceiling of the hotel ballroom with orchids.

So it comes as no surprise to anyone except the father of the bride that the average, no-big-deal wedding these days costs around $30,000. Compared to the S&L bailout, that's not a lot, but it's enough to keep whoever pays for it on macaroni and cheese for a while.

Brides and grooms are assuming more of the cost of their own weddings, not because they're so generous to Daddy, but because they refuse to skimp on the goodies and Daddy can't bury $30,000 in his expense account.

Granted, weddings didn't used to cost so much, but then $30,000 isn't worth what it used to be either. It wasn't long ago that thirty big ones dropped into a presidential campaign would bag you an ambassadorship to some little ole Caribbean country where folks played a lot of golf and drank rum.

So what can you do with thirty grand today? Here's some idea of the purchasing power that weddings generate.

Thirty Thousand Dollars Also Could Buy:
1. A 1,667-year subscription to *Bride's Magazine.*
2. First-class, around-the-world airfare for you, your sweetie and four friends.
3. Tuition from freshman year through doctorate at the University of Minnesota.
4. A Big Mac with fries and a medium drink every day for the next twenty-five years.
5. A BMW 325ic convertible, complete with a compact-disc player and cellular phone.
6. A month of safe shelter, meals and individual counseling for 100 homeless teenagers now living on the streets.
7. Eight pairs of llamas, with enough money left to feed them for their entire twenty-five-year life span.
8. Twelve thousand one hundred ninety-five Dairy Queen Blizzards – enough to treat everybody in my home town of New Ulm, Minnesota, as well as the folks from Hanska, Essig and Klossner.
9. Six snowmobiles with hand and thumb warmers, jackets and helmets – so you, your sweetie, your parents, your in-laws, the best man and the maid of honor all can ride off into the sunset.
10. An acre of ice cream, spread one-half-inch thick.
11. A day's rice for 200,000 children in Bangladesh, or a year's wages for 235 Indian Community Development Project workers building roads, dams and irrigation projects.
12. Five hundred sixty-seven brightly colored bowling balls, personally fitted, with holes drilled and initials engraved on each ball.
13. Two season tickets to the Minnesota Vikings for sixty years, which should *probably* guarantee that you'll be there when they finally win the Super Bowl.
14. Two thousand one hundred forty-four compact discs.
15. Twenty-one Signature series Fender guitars, with enough left over to buy straps.
16. An entire year's perpetual vacation at the best hotel in Cancun.
17. An eighteen-by-thirty-six-foot in-ground pool, with maintenance for thirty years.
18. Down payment on a $300,000 house.
19. A biweekly housecleaning service for twenty-one-and-a-half years.
20. One dozen roses a week for forty-eight years.

GOOSE SAUCE, GANDER SAUCE

A lot of photographers really like posing couples this way for their "Love Story" pictures. (The "Love Story" album is what used to be called the engagement pictures.)

They probably don't consciously decide to make the woman look like a barbarian sex slave in a "Dungeons and Dragons" poster. They probably don't even think it's odd to show her desperately clinging to the nether reaches of a man as if he were her last hope. But if marriage is the meeting of two equals, why do photographers insist on taking pictures in which the bride doesn't even come up to the groom's kneecap?

Wouldn't it make sense to reverse the pose once in a while and let her stand on her own two feet? In a world where we tell women that one size fits all, shouldn't one sauce be good for both the goose and the gander?

Photosymbolism: What Are Your Pictures Saying about You and How Can You Make Them Stop?

Wedding photographs endure. They are a permanent impression of your special day, but they are also a lasting reminder of your level of taste. This is why you need to sit down with your beloved before your wedding day and decide just how much humiliation you can stand in the future.

When your children are going through their nastiest phase, they're going to find your wedding album. Don't you remember how funny you thought your parents' album was?

Even worse – and God forbid that this marriage should not work out – imagine yourself ten years from now seated in your mother's living room, introducing her to your new "special friend." What does Mom do? She goes directly for your first wedding album – the one with your bridal boudoir portrait! Questions of taste can have consequences.

You need to ask what your wedding pictures are going to be saying about you. And it's *you* that they're talking about. It's *your* face in every picture: *You're* the one hoisting your skirt up to flash your gams and garter. *You're* the one double-exposed inside a wedding ring. *You're* the couple looking down on their own ceremony, like ghosts.

It's time to take a romp through the fantasyland of wedding photography.

The Garter Shot

*F*or sheer offensiveness, no wedding photograph beats the garter shot. It's vulgar, rude and often violent in execution. The symbolism is just plain awful – you *know* what Freud said about anything that's round with a hole in it.

The garter shot is the twentieth-century equivalent of hanging the bloody wedding-bed sheets out the window to prove all sorts of stuff to the village. The garter shot is a trophy shot – the cave-man groom is displaying what he's captured to bear children for him. So if it's a trophy shot, let's bloody well make it look like one! Let's require the groom to prove his manly strength by lifting his bride above his head at the wedding.

Hard as it may be to believe, the garter shot is getting worse. The fashion now is for the groom to get down on all fours (doggy-style, as some would say) and take off the garter *with his teeth*. He then throws the garter over his shoulder or shoots it like a rubber band (depending on his emotional age) to the assembled men.

Now the real fun begins. Whoever catches the garter gets to put it on the leg of whoever caught the bouquet. Not just slip it on, but get it as high on her leg as she'll allow. That's a symbol too: the higher the garter goes, the greater the bridal couple's wedded bliss. Hard to find a better alibi than that for playing with someone's leg.

It's only fair to admit that most men realize that this is marginal behavior. When a twelve-year-old or an eighty-year-old catches the bouquet, the guys quietly decide that the newlyweds can take care of their own symbolic happiness.

Maybe the groom ought to wear that garter. Then one of the bridesmaids could try to fit it onto his muscled thighs while the other women hoot encouragement. If nothing else, it would be worth it just to see men blush.

The Consumer Bride

*T*here's a popular shot where the bride holds up her new ring with the reverence of a priest elevating the sacramental host during communion. Now marriage is swell, but let's not get so ambitious in our comparisons. Besides, the picture usually looks less sacramental than mercantile.

Money has always changed hands at weddings because not everybody in the world believes in romance. People believe in getting something tangible when they marry. In New Guinea, for example, a bride can cost upwards of twenty goats. But the money usually flows the other way. Dowries are a loving daddy's bribe to whoever will take a daughter off his hands.

Maybe that's why this picture looks like the documentation of a financial arrangement. So-and-so many ounces of gold and gems have been exchanged for the bride's virtue, fecundity and services. A shrewd bargainer, the bride has overseen and validated the transaction.

But in a post-matrimonial society like ours, the real bride-price isn't paid on the wedding day. The big bills come on the day you get divorced.

Everybody's favorite special effect is the misty image of the bride wistfully thinking of her beloved. That's where the backlit profile of the bride's face fills the right side of the picture and the fully lighted face of the groom is double exposed into the shadows near her ear. This show us that she's thinking about him, because his face is right inside her head where her pituitary gland should be.

Why do they always show the bride? Why not show what's going on in the groom's head? It wouldn't be wistful and soft-focus, and it might be sweaty and bawdy and maybe a little terrified, but hey, it beats being double exposed into the middle of the wedding cake.

SPECIAL EFFECTS AND OTHER TRICKY PIX

Wedding photographers love double exposures because they can cram twice as much into a single frame of film. But you will hurt the photographer's feelings if you call these pictures "trick photos." Photographers call them "special effects," because it sounds more, well, *special*. Sort of like the difference between being kissed by Kathleen Turner or by Nancy Reagan. One's special. The other's just an effect.

Double exposures – oops, sorry – special effects – are supposed to symbolize deep inner meanings, like the picture of the happy couple stuck inside a brandy snifter. Or the moonlit scenic shot where the couple are in heaven where the moon is supposed to be, looking down on us mortals like Aztec Moon Gods.

For further layers of symbolism, you can have the picture mounted and turned into a clock. Or printed on a fine-quality bone-china plate. Or on playing cards. You pays your money and you gets your symbolism.

HE'S GOT HIS BRIDE RIGHT IN HIS HANDS

This is the sort of picture Senator Jesse Helms wants the National Endowment for the Arts to fund. It's a *nice* picture. It's about a man caring for and protecting his womenfolk. It's about chaste, heterosexual, legally married love. It's about a demure woman attending to womanly things like flowers. It's about a godlike male with his woman right in his hands. The only problem with being in someone's hands is that he can crush you so easily if he ever takes a mind to. As far as I can tell, no one has ever photographed the groom's head cradled in his bride's hands. Wouldn't it be truthful to show a bride cradling, nurturing and caring for her husband? Or is the whole darned shot just about power? Some adventurous wedding photographer ought to try displaying a photo like that – I bet lots of people would want to have it in their albums.

STAY MISTY FOR ME

When is a fuzzy picture not just an unfocused dud? When it's supposed to resemble the wedding as seen "Through the Bride's Misty Eyes."

Technically, a soft-focus picture happens whenever you strap a softening filter or device over your lens. As with any technique, the trick isn't in knowing when to use it but in knowing when to stop. It's a lesson not widely learned.

Softening filters were developed to flatter aging movie stars by blurring their wrinkles. Nowadays they're used by wedding photographers to bring romance to familiar places and people by making them nearly impossible to see.

Title Insurance: From Tacky to Tawdry

The person who invents a way of painting wedding photographs directly onto black velvet will create the True American Art Form. Until then, wedding photography will be indebted to wildlife art, also known as art ducko.

Wedding photography and art ducko both present nostalgic, idealized and easily recognizable images. They also share a maddening insistence on sentimental titles. For example: A picture of two ducks landing in a half-frozen slough would be titled "A-coming Home" or maybe "Journey's End," not something too realistic, like "Seconds Away from Getting Their Heads Blown Off."

Wedding photographers are masters of purple prose, particularly at photographic competitions, where they try to impress each other with their sensitivity and creativity but, alas, not their literacy.

Sometimes these titles show with terrifying clarity how wedding photographers view the world and their customers. A picture of the groom alone is titled "Man of the Hour," while the Bride's photograph is titled "Peaches and Creme."

These are genuine wedding photograph titles.

The Title Hall of Shame

"Oooo! Those Legs"
"My Porcelain Bride"
"Our Dream Has Come True"
"This Stairway Will Take Me to Heaven"
"Be Forever Happy, Our Little Angel"
"Angel at the Gate"
"Shower of Romance"
"Canopy of Love"
"Field of Dreams"
"Cathedral Princess"
"Queen for a Day"
"Go Ahead – Kiss Her!"
"Mom's Special Day"
"Gone With the Wind"
"Love Letters in the Sand"
"Cascading Beauty"
"Lisa's Dream"
"Pretty in Peach"
"Greek Goddess"
"Happy Together"
"Treasured Thoughts"
"Interlude At Dusk"

Pictures from an Exhibitionist: Bridal Boudoir Photography

*T*he hottest new trend in photography is boudoir photography, where women dress up in fancy but concealing underwear and have pictures taken for their husbands or boyfriends.

So it stands to reason that the hottest new trend in wedding photography is bridal boudoir photography, which features the same sort of teasing but peculiarly sexless photos. The difference is that in bridal boudoir photography, the model wears frou-frow undies *and* her wedding veil.

Bridal boudoir photography is promoted by photographers as the perfect answer to that nagging question, "What can the bride give the groom that's like, you know, *totally special*?" But they're at pains to point out that it's not so special that it has to be hidden away from children.

The sensuality of boudoir photography isn't on film but in the way the client is treated. The typical boudoir photo session is a half-day of pure pampering. When the woman shows up at the studio, somebody's there to give her a facial. Someone else gives her a manicure. She gets a fancy new hairdo while the make-up woman fusses with her face and gives her personalized beauty tips. There's champagne to be had and soft music wafts gently through the room. By the time the photos start, she's so relaxed she's lucky if she's still in control of her bladder.

Whatever turns your man on, goes. Is your husband the manager of a tire-repair shop? Plunk yourself down on a radial snow tire and cover yourself with a bunch of Goodyear balloons just like Sally Rand. Boyfriend's a football fan? Cut a jersey so it barely covers your chest and get yourself photographed pouting in front of some lockers. Got a hunter hubby? Cover your naughty bits with dead pheasants and get a good grip on his shotgun.

Since both wedding photography and boudoir photography are based on male-generated ideas of female beauty that many women accept wholeheartedly, they're not as contradictory as they might first seem.

Bridal boudoir photography is based on the rule that nothing shows. Everyone involved instinctively *knows* which "nothing" isn't supposed to show and why it matters if it does. The women in the photos are sweet, only selectively available and certainly not aggressive. They're just the girl next door, feeling a little frisky today, and maybe a little sheepish when the four-foot-by-four-foot framed copy arrives.

Now won't *that* be a special gift?

SOMETHING BORROWED, SOMETHING BLUE, SOMETHING UNCONSCIOUS...

It shouldn't have come as any surprise that Kymberli went out like a light when the processional music started. After all, she hadn't eaten for three days because she wanted to look gorgeous in her elegant gown. But on an empty tummy, the champagne she shared with her bridesmaids before the ceremony hit her hard.

Or maybe it was the little tiny tranquilizer Kymberli's mother gave her to settle her nerves that didn't agree with her. But it was only half a pill, and her mom had already taken three with no noticeable effect.

Or it could have been the party the night before. Nobody drank all that much, but they *were* up till 5 A.M., and Kymberli was still sound asleep two hours before the ceremony when her mother splashed water in her face and made her get on her feet.

Some said it was just nerves, and some said with a groom like that they'd faint too and not open their eyes till someone better came along. The doctor said it was just luck that she didn't throw up all over her gown; the minister wanted to know if she was pregnant; her mother came running back up the aisle and broke her heel; and Kymberli – who had dreamed of total perfection for her wedding – just lay there on the floor and didn't care.

The Perfect Day Arrives

*Y*our wedding day is a lot like winning a marathon. There's a heck of a party going on, but you're probably too exhausted to notice.

It's also the day you realize that perfection is just a little joke people play on brides before the wedding. The wedding day is when you get the punch line.

The perfect gown gets fingernail polish on it; the perfect cake arrives the wrong shade; the perfect flowers really were perfect yesterday and would have been perfect today if they had been put in water; the perfect make-up artist leaves you looking embalmed; the perfect hairdo suddenly leaves your veil slip-sliding all over your head.

The perfect unity candle won't light without an acetylene torch; the perfect bridesmaid breaks her leg and shows up in a cast; the perfect best man really can't find the perfect ring; the perfect usher is either potted or has the flu or both; the perfect flower girl has diarrhea; the perfect mother of the bride is a perfect terror.

The perfect air conditioning (or furnace) breaks down; the perfect minister locks himself out of his office and can't get his robes; the perfect groom walks but is otherwise comatose; the perfect soloist is a little flat; the perfect organist speeds up the processional till you're practically jogging; the perfect building next door catches fire and the perfect ceremony is drowned out by fire engines.

The perfect catered meal tastes more like chicken pot-pie than seafood bisque; every perfect guest brings extra, un-RSVPed guests – for whom the caterer is perfectly unprepared; the perfect musicians spend the night playing music no one likes to dance to; the bride's perfect uncle insults the groom's perfect uncle; your perfect going-away clothes get Diet Rite spilled all over them; you keep the perfect limo waiting so long it nearly runs out of gas; and the perfect honeymoon hideaway has no record of your perfect reservation.

In short, the perfect bride is a perfect wreck. Enjoy!

The Perfect Wedding-Not!
True Things That Can and Have Gone Wrong.

*N*o wedding plan survives contact with reality. Brides go into their weddings expecting perfection, and exit glad to have survived.

It's nature's way of reminding us that our wedding is just a time in our lives – not the definitive statement of who we are. If the wedding becomes more important than you, it's time to elope. In the real world, things go wrong, sometimes spectacularly so. It might be helpful to realize that happily married couples have survived each of these marital mishaps without having their relationship ruined. It didn't even ruin the day.

Showers, Parties and General Revels

As anyone who has planned a wedding knows, the fun starts early. So does the funhouse:

"The magazines all said that 'togetherness' was a good thing for couples, so my fiancé and I went roller skating a week before the wedding. He'd never gone roller skating before, so his feet got terribly blistered. Two days later, the blisters got infected, his leg swelled up and he had to hobble around on crutches. Luckily the swelling went down enough before the wedding that he was able to walk on his own. But it didn't go down completely – we had to rent two different sizes of shoes to fit his two different-sized feet."

"I have a world-class Suburban Princess friend who was about to marry a medical doctor with an established practice. There was nothing she needed that we could afford to buy, so her sisters organized a gag shower for her. When we arrived at her house, we were given little foil tiaras and wands. Her artist sister had painted a gaudy diamond ring, matching diamond bracelet and manicured nails onto a pair of latex laundry gloves. I ruined my entire kitchen sprinkling Elmer's Glue and sparkles all over a toilet plunger, and this woman had *no idea* what a toilet plunger was. As every gift was opened, we would all chorus out, 'Oh, that's cute, whaddya pay for that?' We laughed ourselves silly and nobody went to work the next day because we were too exhausted."

The Ceremony

Maybe it's the gravity and solemnity of the ceremony that causes the snafus, or maybe it's the thought that the bride is going to be getting microscopic scrutiny from 300 people, but when something goes astray here, *everybody* notices. So relax. The furnace probably *won't* go out just before your wedding, leaving your visiting Florida relatives shivering in their organdy dresses, but if it does, know that you're not alone.

Ten minutes before her wedding, one bride saw her sweetie and impulsively flipped her dress over her head to show him the garter. Her lipstick smeared all over the front of the dress and she and the bridesmaids went crazy spraying the dress to remove the stain. They did get the lipstick out, but there was a huge wet spot on the front of her dress as she walked down the aisle.

Wedding rehearsals really aren't. At best, you walk through the ceremony in a desultory way and leave without really practicing your cues. At one wedding, the cue for the organist to start the processional was when he saw the mother of the bride enter the church. The priest entered – on cue. The groom's party entered – on cue. But the mother of the bride was nowhere to be seen. After ten minutes, the priest sent an altar boy to find out what the problem was. They wouldn't tell him. After twenty minutes, the priest himself went back to the changing room to find out if perhaps someone was ill. Instead he walked into a raging fight among the women. It seems that the maid of honor had accused the bride of sleeping with the maid of honor's boyfriend the night before. The whole room was full of angry women and it took all of the priest's people skills to calm things down so the wedding could proceed. And it did proceed – forty-five minutes late and with a new maid of honor.

"Years before we met, my hubby had a bizarre fling with a family friend who never forgot him. As a matter of fact, she went around telling everybody that he was a fool not to marry her. Understandably, this woman and I never liked each other. A week before the wedding, she called me up to tell me that she hoped I wouldn't mind if she wore a great new dress she had just found. To get her off the line, I told her to wear whatever she pleased. She showed up at our wedding wearing a floor-length white lace gown. I was so thunderstruck I just started to laugh. I had never been to a wedding before where there were alternate brides."

"My future sister-in-law disliked me so much she showed up at my wedding dressed entirely in black. She didn't say ten words all afternoon – she just stalked around glowering under her black hat and black veil, with her black dress, black gloves and black hose."

"In the weeks before the wedding, one of my least-favorite aunts was being particularly difficult. Her invitation had been delayed briefly in the mail, and now she wanted us to *beg* her to come to the wedding. I was way too busy to beg anybody to come to anything, but I did give her a quick call and she graciously agreed to attend. Something must have upset her between the call and the wedding because when she arrived, she demanded to sit on the groom's side rather than with my family. My family was thrilled, but Doug's family sure got a warped idea of what our family was like."

"You should always have a handkerchief in your sleeve during the wedding. I didn't, and I started to get teary. Then I started to cry. Then I started to *really* cry. And then my nose started to run. Not just a little bit, either, it ran *a lot!* Worst of all, there were two video cameras recording the ceremony, and I look like I'm draining."

"The bridesmaid's gowns the bride had picked out were mauve monstrosities with huge billowed shoulders, a scooped neckline and a plunging back. If I stood very still everything was fine (other than the fact that I looked ridiculous). But as soon as I took a step, those billowing shoulders just billowed right down my arms because my shoulders are narrow. So with the whole congregation watching, I had to walk at half speed down the aisle with my dress falling down. I'd take a step, pause, pull the right shoulder up. Another step, pause, pull the left shoulder up. *All* the way down the aisle. I stayed seated or stationary during the entire reception. The bride was in such a daze she never noticed. In fact, she would rush over every so often and squeal, 'You girls look *so great* in those gowns!'"

"Everybody likes surprises, but not on their wedding day. Without telling me, my fiancé got a perm the day before and showed up with a huge afro-style hairdo. His appearance was so changed that I didn't recognize him when he arrived at the church."

"When my grandmother got married in the 1920s, she asked her best friend to stand up for her. Back then there wasn't much fuss made about coordinating the wedding, so my grandmother never inquired what dress her friend might wear. The friend was quite a seamstress, though, and she went to a department store, saw a dress she liked and copied it from memory. I guess Grandma should have described her dress, because when the maid of honor showed up at the wedding, she was wearing a homemade version of the same dress my grandmother had bought. Grandma said she never had much to do with that woman after that."

People faint at weddings. The clothes are usually too tight, people are nervous, they lock their knees standing at the altar and next thing you know, they're history. Brides faint, grooms faint, mothers, fathers, grandmothers, ushers and flower girls faint. Even ministers faint. One minister dropped during the ceremony and no one knew whether he was alive or dead. The congregation finally managed to revive him and he finished the ceremony.

The unity candle is a symbol that is bound to go wrong. Sometimes the mothers can't get the family candles to light. More often the unity candle won't light and occasionally the priest just has to flick his Bic and blast that wick. Even that isn't enough at times and the candle can keep extinguishing itself throughout the service, to horrible symbolic effect. If it does stay lit, the symbolism can still go astray if the acolyte doesn't think before he just snuffs the candle in front of the assembled guests. You've got to be very careful about symbolism that can boomerang in public.

"I should have listened to the omens at my first wedding. The night before the wedding the snow turned to rain and covered everything with solid ice. People who had traveled 300 miles through snow couldn't get six blocks from their motel rooms to the church. One of the attendants fell down and broke his wrist, and a guest broke her hip on the steps outside the church. After the service, we were trying to take some pictures of my husband and me at the altar when my veil caught on fire. He just stared at me as if to say, 'Hey – your head's on fire!'"

With all the premarital counseling required before a wedding nowadays, the old "Speak now or forever hold your peace" clause is seldom put to the congregation. Maybe it should be. Recently, as one minister was about to pronounce the couple husband and wife, an enraged woman came storming down the aisle, dragging her pregnant daughter behind her. The minister called for time out and took the couple into his office. It seems that the groom had indeed been intimate with the woman's daughter. In fact, he had tried to marry her, but the mother wouldn't allow someone of his "ethnic background" to marry her daughter. The bride was aware of the controversy, as were all four parents. What's an officiant to do? With no moral or legal obstacles to the current marriage, he went ahead and married them after a hour's delay. Pity the poor organist who had to ad lib an hour's worth of music while the battle raged in the pastor's office.

"The only time I really wanted to catch the bouquet was at my sister's wedding. I went for it, but another woman wanted it a lot more. She not only knocked me out of the way, but when we both came down, I had a couple of her false fingernails in my hand. The curse must have worked, because I'm still not married four years after it happened!"

Weddings can be dangerous to your health. File this new paranoia under "P," as in "Parasitic Pigeon Poop Pops 'em as Positive-thinking Pastor Protests Painful Publicity." It seems that 130 people who went to two outdoor weddings at a popular amphitheater one fine June day came down with a mystery disease, which turned out to be the result of a parasitic fungus spread by bird droppings. A freak occurrence, but the publicity nearly ruined the church's rental schedule and particularly perturbed the previously placid pastor.

It was the bride's second wedding and she wanted her three-year-old daughter to be the flower girl. But three is too young for that kind of pressure, and halfway down the aisle the girl stopped dead in her tracks and upended her entire basket of flower petals. The bride just took her daughter's hand and walked down the aisle with her bouquet in one arm and the girl on the other.

Singers

Wedding guests are a captive audience, and some singers ought to be reported to Amnesty International. It's pretty hard to avoid noticing a problem when it's off-key on the public address system.

The bride was the church soloist and wanted to sing at her own wedding. As she entered on her father's arm, she stopped halfway down the aisle and sang "I'd Rather Have Jesus." Talk about putting the groom on notice.

"We were married right after college graduation and had asked an old friend from high school to sing. Unfortunately, we hadn't heard him sing in four years and weren't aware how much his voice had deepened. He asked the organist to transpose one song down half an octave, but she got flustered and played it in the original key, leaving a painful sixteen-bar silence where he couldn't reach the notes. We were trapped on our knees at the altar, unable to turn around to see what the problem was for the longest sixteen bars of our lives."

Don't leave anything to chance with your soloist. You might get all seventy-four verses of a song – all slightly off-key. One soloist tried but the longer he sang, the slower he got. Finally, as the soloist took a breath, the minister just started talking. The singer never did finish that song.

"My mother decided that it would be a great idea if my aunt would sing at our wedding. But auntie had a voice that sounded like a hog being tortured, and was tone deaf to boot. We realized we couldn't keep her from singing entirely, so we compromised and asked her to sing a 'special solo' to open the reception. That way, the laughter didn't seem so out of place."

The Clergy

From the clergy's standpoint, marriage is only one of several sacraments, but it certainly causes the most problems. When was the last time you heard about someone collapsing in tears because their daughter's baptism didn't go perfectly?

"The first wedding I ever performed I was in a panic, worried that I'd mess something up. But everything went very well till the end. I pronounced them husband and wife and they left the altar, followed by the attendants. Relieved, I started down the aisle with vigor – but without having unplugged my neck mike. I nearly strangled myself."

"Our minister got locked out of church office because the assistant pastor had taken the keys. All of his vestments were in the office and it was too late to call a locksmith or anyone else with keys. Luckily, our minister is a former football player and he just kicked in the door."

"Our pastor used our premarital counseling sessions mostly to harangue us because we interpreted some scriptures differently than he did. To avoid unpleasantness at the ceremony, we asked him not to use the 'wives submit to your husbands' passage. At our wedding he not only disregarded our wishes, he really dug in his heels and went on at length about submission and obedience. I was holding my husband's hand and we both started clenching our fists so hard I thought my nails were going to draw blood. I can't say I was surprised a year and a half later when I heard that his own wife had left him and had taken refuge in a shelter for battered women."

"I had to officiate at a small wedding for two nineteen-year-olds who had been partying far too heartily the night before. An hour before the wedding, the bride was still sound asleep. Her mother got her up, splashed water in her face, got her into her gown and brought her to the church. No one in the wedding party looked particularly healthy. Halfway through the ceremony, the bride pitched forward and whispered, 'I'm not going to make it.' I grabbed her, hissed, 'Not here,' and scooted her behind a potted plant, where I held her head while she relieved herself. I thought I had saved the day. Then I stood up and realized that my microphone had been live the entire time and I had broadcast the whole episode."

"We're a small, rural church deep in the north woods, so it didn't seem too odd when one of my parishioners asked me to officiate at a black-powder wedding. The groom and all the men were outfitted in buckskin frontier garb with flintlock rifles. There was even a little black-powder cannon which scared the tar out of the mother of the groom. When it came time to exchange the rings, the best man put on a thick leather glove with a hunk of meat on it and waved his arm in the air. A falcon was supposed to deliver the ring, but on the way, the falcon spotted a tasty little bird and took off after it. When he finally did arrive, the ring was way too bloody to use."

The Reception

The reception is the biggest party you'll ever throw, but probably not the most decorous. There have been receptions where the mother of the bride and the mother of the groom got into a fight with broken bottles on the dance floor because they disagreed about what music the DJ was supposed to play. And there have been weddings where the bride's family limited itself to inviting twenty-five relatives, while 275 relatives (mostly uninvited) of the groom showed up. They ate and drank everything in sight, then ran out to liquor store, bought more and presented the father of the bride with the receipt and demanded to be repaid on the spot.

Young women have never been more athletic than they are today, but no game teaches you how to throw something over your shoulder. Being athletic just gives you a better arm, so that now when the bouquet toss goes wrong, it goes very wrong. Bouquets have gone straight up, hitting the bride on their way down. They have landed in punch bowls and gotten hopelessly snagged in chandeliers. They're terrible predictors of symbolic fertility, having been caught by nuns, dogs, grade-school girls and, on at least one occasion, a six-year-old boy. He didn't actually catch it. He more or less got hit by it and just held on. When he heard what catching the bouquet meant, he shrieked and threw it, fearful that he had caught girl germs.

Whether your cake releases doves when you cut into it or the icing is so hard that it has to be taken back to the kitchen for the groom to cut it with a hunting knife, cakes can make a contribution to your wedding woes. Cakes usually cause a scandal by their absence or their premature destruction. Wedding cakes have toppled over into small children who are sneaking a sample of frosting and have missed the wedding altogether when the chef took a shortcut through a corn field and got stuck up to her hub caps.

The couple had rented the reception hall – a gorgeous old home with many rooms on two floors and a complex layout – for an afternoon wedding. As the staff was getting ready for the evening reception, they discovered the three-year-old ring boy asleep on an upstairs couch. The only phone number the staff had was the bride and groom's apartment, and no one was there. So they started calling everybody with the bride's last name in the phone book. Eventually, they got the ring boy's mother. When they told her that her son was asleep at their hall, all she could say was "Oh, my God...Oh, my God...Oh, my God...." Everybody had assumed that the boy had gone home with someone else.

The best thing about wedding catastrophes is that most of them can be easily remedied. An inebriated guest once stumbled and put his hand through a wedding cake. The photographer simply turned the cake around and sent his assistant to the drug store for a can of shaving cream. He then filled the hole with shaving cream and told the bride not to serve from the bottom layer. No problem!

Fainting, Throwing Up and Changing Your Mind

Not every marriage is made in heaven and not every woman is hell-bent on getting married. At least, not on marrying this particular guy.

Getting married is an awesome step. You're committing yourself to a lifetime (or several years, whichever works out best) of pantyhose drying in the shower, power saws left all over the garage floor and a whole loony bin of in-laws and offspring who are only going to get stranger in the future.

Everybody has some wedding-day jitters. But if you lose consciousness, you need either to rethink your wedding plans or check yourself into a good chemical-abuse treatment center. So when do you know when you should signal for time out and run off the field? Here are some hints.

When Should You Call Off the Wedding?

1. When you are still downstairs throwing up fifteen minutes before the ceremony, you should listen to your feelings, particularly when nausea is the only feeling you're feeling.

2. When neither you, your parents nor your attendants can stop crying every time you think about the wedding, it's time to cancel. This is particularly true when it's the men who are all sobbing uncontrollably.

3. When the bride is more attracted to the best man than the groom, it's time for a reality check. If the bride is more attracted to her bridesmaids than to the groom, either she will have to raise her consciousness or he will have to lower his expectations.

4. When the officiant says, "You may kiss the bride," and she says to the groom, "It's been a wonderful evening; let's not spoil it now," you may want to sign up for a little counseling.

5. When the bride comes to the altar and says under her voice, "Well, look who's finally ready to make a commitment – old Bozo himself," you should remember that sarcastic couples seldom celebrate their fiftieth anniversaries together.

M.O.B. Rule: The Mother of All Brides

*T*he bride only *appears* to be the central figure of the wedding. The mother of the bride is the true center. The bride's only along for the ride, just as her mother was at her own wedding decades ago. That wedding was run by the bride's grandmother. Now the mother of the bride is going to show both her daughter and her own mother how to do this thing right!

Despite what many brides think, a wedding does not change a mother's character, although it *does* reveal it more clearly. Sometimes it reveals a woman's true character so convincingly that it's years before the family is on speaking terms again.

Of course, there is an infinite variety of mothers involved in weddings, but here are three of the most frequently encountered personality types. They are The String Puller, a woman with what they call "control issues"; The Wanna-Be, who hates sharing the spotlight; and The Weeper, who says that she cries because she's happy, which suggests that she gets CNN confused with the Comedy Channel.

It's possible that the mother of the groom shares these emotions, but nobody has ever thought to ask. Being the mother of the groom is like appearing in someone else's dream. It's flattering to be thought of, but it's not the sort of experience you remember a lot about later.

M.O.B. #1: The Weeper

Women don't cry at weddings because they're happy. They cry because they're terrified. They're in the middle of an emotional earthquake. The wedding is the epicenter and it's right under the mother of the bride. The primary event doesn't last long, but when it's over her life has been rearranged and all her china is in a heap on the floor.

There's no force in nature that can shatter a family's old certainties about status, control and sex more thoroughly than a wedding. The bride and groom are oblivious to the tremors, but their parents feel every aftershock. It's the parents who lose control over their little girl or darling son. It's the parents whose status downsizes from Lord and Lady of the Manor to overnight guests at a newlywed's apartment. And it's the parents who have to – gasp, gag, spit – come to grips with the undeniable fact that their baby is engaging in all sorts of S.E.X.! No wonder the mother of the bride is bawling her eyes out. She knows that she's not losing a daughter, she's gaining a son. Worse yet is the knowledge that most brides marry a man similar to their own fathers.

The mother of the groom should be crying too, but she's saving her tears because she knows that a daughter is a daughter all her life long, but a son is a son till he's married, and then he's an S.O.B.

M.O.B. #2: The String Puller

The downside of maternal bonding is that the greater the bonding, the more strings there are left over to pull. And nowhere do those strings get pulled in such an orchestrated frenzy as they do at a wedding.

The wedding may be the bride's party, but the mother of the bride is the official hostess. If that seems inconsequential, remember that Nancy Reagan was "just" the official hostess at the White House.

A daughter *owes* her mother her wedding. Momma had to have *her* mother's wedding twenty-five years ago and she's been fuming about it for a quarter of a century. That's a long time to plan and get your mind set. Certainly it's too long to tolerate any backtalk from some young whippersnapper.

Cheat your mother out of your wedding and she'll haunt you for life. And beyond. This is what tradition means: it ain't a tradition unless you have no choice in the matter.

Any woman who wants to run a wedding to her own taste needs to be an independently wealthy orphan or plan on having daughters.

M.O.B. #3: The Wanna-Be

In today's world, weddings are coequally planned by two adult women who are best friends and who just *happen* to be related. Of course, anyone could tell they're related because they're so attractive that you can't tell the mother from the daughter. So they're planning a party at which one of them will be treated like a goddess come to earth and the other will be treated, well...with respect. Like the respect you give a beautifully burnished grandfather clock that's stopped running but still has lots of sentimental value.

And who wouldn't want to be the center of attention at a wedding? People rush to tell the bride that she's never looked lovelier. And well she should – she's wearing a gown that someone else paid thousands and thousands of dollars for. Everyone tells the bride she's radiant, that she's a beauty to behold, that her hair is perfect, her skin is peaches and cream, her figure a delight.

Do they tell the mother of the bride that she's the most stunning thing to walk the face of the earth? No, all she hears is that she ought to be proud to have raised a perfect daughter. And by the way, how's your tennis elbow – or is it arthritis now?

It's not the bride who needs the flattery. It's the mother of the bride who desperately needs a few strokes. She's the one who's terrified that now, with her daughter married and gone, she'll have to start to wear head scarves, thick stockings and galoshes like a Russian peasant.

Who wouldn't want to trade places?

The Father of the Bride: The Invisible Man

Saying that the father of the bride is the second most important man in the wedding ceremony should be quite a compliment, but somehow it isn't.

Other famous second-most-important men include Dan Quayle, Spiro Agnew, "Cactus Jack" Garner and Hannibal Hamlin, who, as you may recall, was the vice-president who *didn't* succeed Abraham Lincoln.

Being father of the bride is the worst blow possible to a male ego. In the Dark Ages, unfortunate wretches had to give the headsman a coin before he chopped off their heads. Nowadays the father of the bride has to give *all* his coins to the caterers, florists and so on, just to publicly announce that he is so old that he is less than a year away from becoming a grandfather. It's bad enough to lose a daughter, but to lose your youthful vigor on the same day is too much!

American males are used to getting all the attention when they pay for something. A wedding is like buying a round of drinks that nobody notices. Too old to throw a tantrum to draw attention to themselves, some men resort to petty misdemeanors, like getting drunk and breaking plates, or posing with their pants pockets pulled out to show that they're broke.

No matter how sorry the father of the bride may feel for himself, the truly invisible man of the wedding is the father of the groom. That poor dude could show up in a full body cast and nobody would notice.

For those fathers of the bride who do not wish to go softly into that good night, here are some ways you can make yourself totally noticed at your daughter's wedding.

At the Ceremony
1. Wear a tux that's color coordinated to match the bridesmaids' dresses.
2. When you "give away" the bride, give her a noticeable shove toward the groom, to make her new status obvious to everyone.
3. Just before the bride enters, stop the ceremony till the congregation has recited the Pledge of Allegiance.
4. Read *The Prophet* from the lectern and break down sobbing. Go into a rambling discourse about what this means to you as an Adult Child of Whatever-kind-of-parents.
5. Blow your nose loudly when it comes time for your daughter to say "I do."

At the Reception

1. Lead the bridal party in dancing the hora, but only if your family is Episcopalian.
2. Forget the groom's name while offering a toast.
3. Start a food fight.
4. Sing "Feelings," or maybe "Sunrise, Sunset."
5. Open your daughter's wedding presents at the reception and loudly announce the dollar value of each. You could even make a chart.
6. Announce that you are leaving the bride's mother to move in with a male lover.
7. Accuse the father of the groom of trying to sneak a case of champagne into his car trunk.
8. Tell everybody you're glad your daughter got an abortion when she got pregnant three years ago so she didn't have to marry *that* loser.
9. Grab your nephew's skateboard, go down the front steps and break your leg. When the medics come, insist on an air cast and refuse to go to the hospital. Spend the rest of the night telling everybody that nothing would keep you from enjoying your daughter's wedding.
10. Tell everyone you hope they enjoy the reception because the dinners cost $64.75 each, no-shows included.

F.O.B. #1: The Clown

Jerry Lewis was America's most popular comedian when the fathers of today's brides were impressionable young men, which may explain why they now act like such nincompoops at their daughters' weddings.

The problem is that they're still stuck in those old Jerry Lewis movies, particularly during solemn times when they feel vaguely out of place.

Like weddings, for example. Men live their lives going through the motions of being an adult. They pay for what they're supposed to pay for without complaining. They get fitted for a tuxedo, although they promised at their senior prom they'd never do it again. They rehearse the ceremony and perform the ceremony and make a reasonably adult toast to the new couple without having their voices crack.

But then someone puts them on the spot – suddenly it's time for a bit of mature wit, something sardonic but not cynical, something memorable that the family will treasure for years. What do they do? Their thin veneer of sophistication shatters and they're ten-year-olds mimicking Jerry Lewis again. They pull out their pockets!

But with any luck, the women in their lives won't notice because they're role-playing Tammy or Gidget or Doris Day by looking appropriately misty, wistful and dewy-young. We love our spouses almost as much as we love our role models.

What a nutty situation!

F.O.B. #2: The Attention Grabber

Some men can't stand it when they're not the center of attention. At a basketball game, they want to be the forward. At a funeral, they want to be the corpse. And at their daughter's wedding, watch out! These guys aren't hard to locate. They're former high school quarterbacks who still have their press clippings readily available. They're the guys who frame the certificates of attendance from every in-house training seminar they've ever attended. They're the M.D.s who drive sports cars with vanity license plates and park wherever they damned well please.

These are men who thrive on attention. They're used to doing whatever needs to be done to get that attention, whether it's humiliating nurses to make themselves look good or framing "Famous People Who Have Known Me" pictures of themselves shaking hands with celebrities.

Subtlety has never been their strong point, nor has consistency. What better way to upstage a room full of soft organ music than to grab a bagpipe and lead the procession into the church! Whether or not the father of the bride is a Scotsman has nothing to do with it. The point is that he's brought the attention back to its rightful owner – himself.

He's not losing a daughter, he's regaining his audience.

F.O.B. #3: The Coach

Football provides the Great American Male Role Model, defining men's goals and self-perceptions. Young boys want to be flamboyant, outrageous superstars, daily doing derring-do deeds and shooting their mouths off in public. As men grow older, they realize the only position they'll ever get to play is linebacker, destroying their bodies time after time to make their bosses look like heroes.

But the ultimate and most lasting role an American male aspires to is that of The Coach. The Coach is in total control – a silent, brooding presence, emotionally disconnected from the tumult of the game. The all-knowing Coach dispatches his players with fairness and wisdom. They disobey him at their peril. All The Coach has to do to maintain appearances is to keep from scratching himself on national TV.

It's no wonder that the father of the bride feels like a coach. Coaches *used* to be superstars at the center of attention. But they're on the sidelines now, serving in an advisory capacity to a bunch of young bucks. Through it all, The Coach never lets his emotions show. He watches the clock run out and knows the rules: Don't flinch, don't cry and don't scratch.

Forget John Wayne! The great American male metaphor is The Coach: emotionally distant, uncommunicative, all-powerful and stoic. Being the father of the bride is a lot like coaching the Denver Broncos in the Super Bowl. It's a nice honor, but the day will wear you out.

DANCING CHEEK TO CHEEK AND HEAD TO HEAD

For a truly memorable wedding dance, make sure your DJ is prepared for the Reindeer Dance. If your wedding guests are the kind who drink their champagne (or beer) out of paper cups to add fiber to their diet, they'll love the Reindeer Dance!

When the DJ announces the Reindeer Dance, the floor clears of the halt, lame and aged, and the DJ puts on the wildest music he can find. Then all the young bucks in your wedding party pick up their folding chairs, put them over their heads, stomp onto the dance floor and butt each other.

The Department of Natural Resources claims this is a perfectly safe practice, and several hunters groups say it is beneficial in thinning the herd. There has been no comment from the animal-rights organizations.

Dances with Brides: The Epic Reception

Some people see their wedding receptions as a chance to show their friends a good time. Others see the reception as their friends' chance to show them a good time. These practical folks know that the reception is costing them $75 per head, and they have no intention of losing money on the evening. Cash, not gadgetry, is the wedding gift of choice. If the Federal Reserve had a bridal registry, they'd be on it.

If you've been invited to one of these money-market receptions, you are expected to bring a free-will (cash) wedding offering of at least $150. This will cover the bride and groom's out-of-pocket expenses and assure a decent return on their investment. If you're coming with a guest under this plan, expect to shell out $250. You really can't afford to bring the whole family.

Eventually weddings and receptions will be brought into line with standard Wall Street practices. There will be no wedding announcement, just a press release announcing the coming merger, acquisition or hostile takeover of one partner.

The wedding will be formalized by the Securities and Exchange Commission and the reception will be eliminated because the business of business is to make deals, not to provide goods and services to just anybody. Receptions are notorious loss centers because of their overstaffing, lack of productivity and poorly defined goals for the work group.

In the meantime, forward-thinking couples can downscale the reception to include just themselves. Then, with a good billing system for their home computer, they can invoice instead of inviting people. The statement could be personalized by enclosing a photograph with a note: "Hi – Harry and I are getting married. You're single, so please remit $75. If you've found a boyfriend since we talked a month ago, please remit $150. Any account more than thirty days overdue will be assessed a 1.5% service fee."

This system would be cheaper for the guests, lower the bride and groom's overhead and secure a more certain profit for the happy couple. A truly sentimental touch would be to include a tiny airline bottle of Scotch, just enough to provide each account receivable with a hangover. After all, isn't that what wedding receptions are all about?

Wedding Dances as Tribal Fertility Rites

*A*wedding is a wedding is a wedding, but a reception is a *party!* That's how it works the world over, from Malawi to New Jersey, Macedonia to Minnesota.

Every wedding is a sign that the human race is starting over. Maybe this will be the time a couple gets it right: They'll learn, love and stay together. There'll be babies who are wanted and who will grow up strong and wise. That's something to celebrate.

Another constant is relatives. Try to remember that other people have relatives too, some of them so embarrassing that they think *your* family is tolerable.

Let's look at a typical wedding-reception guest list – just a couple of nice, all-American families – which may explain why people try to move as far from their families as possible when they get married.

The Elders

Grandma has been on Meals on Wheels for a little over a year now, so she was in heaven at the wedding reception. Everything the caterers served was on her doctor's forbidden list, or was at least something that Meals on Wheels never serves.

Grandpa wasn't as enthused. He's never been totally comfortable with any vegetable you don't mash before serving, and the artichoke appetizers caught him by surprise.

The Juniors

Shelly, age 9, thinks that weddings would be a lot more fun if no boys were invited, particularly her cousin Brandon. She is very concerned about boy germs, a fear that isn't helped by watching the public-service announcements on TV.

Brandon, age 6, thought it was radical to be the ring bearer, but nature called just before the processional and Brandon came running down the aisle, tucking in his shirt, with the ring pillow clenched in his teeth. Everybody thought that was cute except Shelly, who hit Brandon with her flower basket when no one was looking.

The Aunts at the Picnic

Aunt Maureen is a bubbling wellhead of misinformation, disinformation and unsupported conclusions. An observer of the human condition, she points out that you can observe a lot just by watching. Her key to understanding people: "Once you find out what someone's phobias are, you can tell right away what they're afraid of!" Maureen loved the wedding. It went so well that it was "just like falling off a piece of cake," and the soloist was so good, she told her sister, that "there wasn't a dry seat in the church."

Auntie Ann, the family flirt, has always enjoyed flirting because it amuses the men and irritates the women. The family still hasn't recovered from the time Ann advised one of the nephews to get a girlfriend instead of a motorcycle because no one ever got killed falling off a lover.

Aunt Barbara and Uncle Tim showed up just to prove that you can have all the answers even if you aren't thoughtful enough to ask any interesting questions. Since their college days of hot-tub cannabis parties, Tim and Barb have turned quite religious. No one wants to sit next to Barb because she never shuts up about how the Second Coming is coming in the year 2000. Barb is proof perfect that large round numbers have an unsettling effect on the undisciplined mind.

Cry Uncle

Uncle Henry took time away from his easy-listening radio station to come to the wedding, although he left the reception early. Black coffee and regular radio stations both make him jittery, so he always has decaf radio playing in his car and his kitchen. He's comfortable only with announcers whose voices are so soothing that they sound like they're trying to talk someone out of taking hostages. It's hard to relax around a man who needs such constant soothing.

Uncle "Where's the Bar?" Fred told everyone that he came back early from his island vacation just to go to the wedding. What he failed to mention was that he left after drinking 190 bottles of beer in six and a half days, depleting the resort's liquor supply. The next shipment wasn't due for three days, so Fred packed up his wife and left.

Uncle Dave treats his car like a beloved child and assumes that all his wife and children need is an annual tune-up. He recently moved to Arizona because he couldn't wash his car every day during Minnesota winters. In Minnesota, he took great pride on his pure black wintertime driveway: He would snowblow the driveway, shovel it, then sweep it. When he came home, he would stop the car in the street to kick off the ice chunks. Dave never could stand the thought of snow clinging to his tires and invading his clean garage.

Dave thinks he is being witty when he refers to his first wife as only a "test bride." Every woman in the family is convinced that Dave is just the type to drop bits of thread around the house to make sure his wife vacuums the floor properly.

HOLD YOUR RECEPTION IN HISTORIC HERBERT HOOVER COUNTRY!

America's coming back home in the nineties, and it's hard to get more back home than Wilton Junction, Iowa, where the fortunate bride can hold her reception at the International Ballroom and Feed Shack.

The International Ballroom isn't named in honor of any nearby foreign countries. The International Ballroom used to be an International Harvester tractor dealership, and if the rural economy ever recovers, it's darned well going to be a tractor dealership again.

What was left after the last combine was shipped back to the factory was a huge building with a good concrete floor that was perfect for dances. The Feed Shack restaurant, specializing in *cuisine du fermier* (farmer food), will cater the whole event for you and even serve liquor. Even though most of the receptions held at the International Ballroom are from the Methodist church down the road, only one wedding party has ever asked that no alcohol be served, Methodist or no. Church is church and weddings are weddings, but a reception is a *party!*

You won't find any better place between West Branch and Bettendorf to hold your wedding reception than the International Ballroom and Feed Shack!

Wedding Gifts and Why You Have to be Nice about Them

*W*edding presents aren't exactly bribes, but in today's economy, withholding them can be a pretty good threat. Wedding gifts are society's way of making sure you get married properly and to the right person. If you live with someone, distant relatives will not buy you microwaves. If you marry someone your family dislikes, you will get only a couple of hand towels and some placemats. If you marry someone of your own gender, some of your relatives may break into your house and take back the presents they gave you for high school graduation.

On the other hand, some people forget that, besides being a sacrament and all, weddings are about the orderly transition of large sums of money. Faced with the joy of a new in-law, their minds come unhinged and they decide that what the newlyweds really want and need is something *personal* – something they themselves personally have made.

Personal things tend to hang on a wall. String art, religious decoupage and crafts projects hang on walls. So do amateur watercolors and sensitive black-and-white photos of backlit dandelions.

Flemish tapestries and investment-grade Impressionist paintings also hang on walls, but very few of us have relatives who give that kind of wedding present.

You have to be polite about whatever you get, because if you're not, people won't buy you a wedding present the next time you get married

Worst Possible Wedding Gifts

An informal poll turned up these wedding gifts that someone or other had received in good faith. Virtually none of them were recyclable, returnable or reusable as gifts at another wedding.

1. An enameled, brass unicorn doorstop.
2. Brass mugs shaped like cuspidors and engraved with the couple's names.
3. A four-foot-tall plaster fork-and-spoon wall hanging.
4. Industrial-strength twin turtledove pomanders that smelled like urinal disinfectants.
5. A towel, hand towel and washcloth set for one person.
6. A velvet painting of Elvis and Jesus walking into the sunset.
7. A five-foot, stuffed and wall-mounted sailfish.
8. A complete set of *Reader's Digest* Condensed Books.
9. A large book of erotic art, given by one of the groom's former lovers.
10. A sterling silver ashtray that looked like a barbecue grill.

Thank-You Notes

Thank-you notes are the ransom you pay for all the goodies you get at your wedding. They are also the first realization the new bride has of what a nincompoop she married. George Bush probably spent his honeymoon writing thank-you notes, but most men are barely capable of licking stamps.

This is because most wedding presents don't ring a guy's chimes. How many men give a flying rat's snout whether or not you got all twelve place settings of Royal Dingdong silver plate? Like most men, I knew where babies came from in grade school, but I had no idea where forks came from until I wandered into Louis Drugstore in Sioux Falls, South Dakota, during my sophomore year in college. There, spread before me, was a whole bin of forks, another of spoons and so on. Mother had never told me where flatware came from, so after that I assumed that everybody had to drive out to Sioux Falls to buy their forks. That didn't make sense, but then the first explanation of sex I heard didn't make a lot of sense either.

Most men make the mistake of thinking that their brides are so thrilled about being married that they won't mind writing all the thank-you notes. This is dangerous and will come back to haunt them. The problem with thank-you notes is that they are the most mind-numbing business short of assembly-line work. You've got this little-bitty space on the card to fill up with insincerities as well as specifically identify the item about which you are fibbing. A typical woman's note would look like this:

Dear Aunt Sara,
Thank you so much for the wonderful place setting of Garden Apartment china. It's just perfect for entertaining! We'll treasure it always!
Love, Betsi

If men wrote notes, they'd sound the way men talk, which is why a lot of women don't trust their new husbands anywhere near the stationery:

Hey Sara,
Thanks for the plates. They're round and flat, just like plates are supposed to be. We'll think of you every time we use them until we break them, and then we'll think about your divorce.
Don't be a stranger!

Truth is a wonderful thing, but it has no place in thank-you notes. All the same, it's fun to think what you could say if you were allowed to be really, really honest.

Dear Joan,
We couldn't believe you'd part with the money to buy a whole place setting of Royal Dingdong silver plate. You must have been so rushed that you couldn't even get to the crafts store to buy another plaster grape-cluster candle sconce like you got my sister, Cheryl.
Thanks oodles!

Dear Bill and Margie,
Thanks for the gold-plated serving dish. Where'd you get this thing? You're too old to spend much time at county fairs. Bill — my wife thinks that you got it as a door prize down at that lodge of yours where you wear those funny clothes and won't let minorities or women join. I think you got it out of a dumpster.
Write and let us know!

Dear Mr. & Mrs. Thompson,
Thanks for the extremely large wall hanging. We've already given it away to someone with even less taste than you, though God knows it was hard to find someone like that. Luckily, you're my dad's business associate (and he thinks you're an idiot too) so you'll never be invited into our home to see if we still have your travesty.
Don't call us, we'll call you.

Dear Tom,
What is this? A serving fork from someone with your money? What did you tell the IRS you spent on our present? Heads up, doghead — I have a copy disk of your billing hours at the firm and I can point out discrepancies that would sink even a full partner.
Yours in equitable service.

Dating a Wedding by Multiple Gifts

Wedding gifts are touchstones of a time. They're the trendy items of the day. Sometimes an item will get so trendy that half of your wedding guests buy it for you. Then *you* have to decide how many salad shooters one household really needs.

Multiple wedding gifts are the carbon dating of wedding archeology. You can tell when someone was married by asking which gifts they got in multiples. For example, people who got married in the 1970s are still trying to give away all the Crockpots they received, but if a bride wants a Crockpot nowadays, she'll have to buy herself one, if she can find it.

What are the trendy items to look for when dating gifts? Here's a chart that might help:

1930s
- Depression glass – *you didn't buy it, you got it at the movies.*
- Coffee pots – *the big ones that could water most of the garden.*
- Dish towels – *made from flour sacks.*

1940s
- Hand eggbeaters – *for scrambled eggs. Soufflés didn't come from Victory Gardens.*
- Kitchen clocks – *practically the only thing with a motor you could get during the war.*

- Hammered-aluminum cake plates with glass covers – *for cakes worthy of being displayed, made from scratch!*

1950-1955
- Fiesta Ware.
- Casseroles with heating candles.
- Carpet sweepers.
- Milk-glass serving sets.
- Irons, toasters, deep-fat fryers – *or any of the appliances unavailable during the war.*
- Hand-cranked ice cream makers.
- Bath towels and sheets – *also unavailable during the war.*

1955-1960
- Electric blankets and nylon comforters.
- Lazy Susans – *with individual serving compartments.*
- Sequined felt covers – *for the TV Guide or phone book.*
- Electric "The Bar is OPEN" signs – *for the bar in your basement rec room.*
- Wooden salad bowls and napkin rings – *from the Philippines.*
- Corningware – *tuna con carne hotdish from the oven to the table!*
- Matching sets of hostess hand towels.

1960-1965

- Electric toothbrushes.
- Teflon anything.
- Waring Blenders – *for mixed drinks with tiny umbrellas.*
- Copper-bottomed Revere Ware – *back when women stayed home to polish copper.*
- Bar-b-que grills – *with rotisserie motors, hoods and matching utensils.*
- TV trays – *furniture that doesn't detract from TV dinners.*
- Melmac – *place settings that don't detract from TV trays.*
- Turquoise or pink bath towels.

1965-1970

- Wood cutting boards and hand-thrown pots – *natural products for natural couples.*
- Stash boxes – *for natural couples getting a little unnatural on occasion.*
- Pepper mills – *the bigger the better, just like in fancy Italian restaurants.*
- Steak-knife sets – *remember steak? It came with potatoes before cholesterol and animal rights.*
- Lava lamps – *before they returned as cumpy/trendy "cultural references."*
- Avocado or Harvest Gold bath towels.

1970-1975

- Fondue sets and Crockpots
- Stained-glass window hangings.
- Pewter plates with sayings – *the corporate residue of the youth revolution.*
- Hibachi grills – *for those romantic nights when it didn't matter if you couldn't grill for more than two people at a time.*
- Mugs – *with clever sayings.*
- Peter Max print bath towels.

1975-1980

- Unicorn sculptures – *and "sculpted" candles taller than your dog.*
- Electric can openers.
- Woks – *electric, stove-top and barbecue.*
- Pasta machines.
- Chicago Cutlery.
- Single-patty electric hamburger friers.
- Fry Daddy and Fry Baby fat friers – *just listen to them arteries snap shut!*
- Toaster ovens.
- Mugs – *with clever cartoons.*
- Earth-tone bath towels.

1980-1985

- Depression glass and Fiesta Ware – *again.*
- Yogurt makers and food dryers – *gotta stay healthy in the coming apocalypse!*
- Ice-cream maker – *electric, not hand-cranked.*
- Cuisinarts – *the Waring Blender of the Eighties.*
- Romertopf cookware – *slow cooking for fast status.*
- Digital clocks – *waking up to microchips.*
- Mugs – *with French engravings.*
- Matching monogrammed shower robes.

1985-1990

- Krups coffee grinders and espresso machines – *caffeine becomes America's recreational drug of choice.*
- Calphalon – *heavy-gauge anodized-aluminum professional cookware for the new, lighter cuisine.*
- Electric juicers – *all-natural, half the work.*
- Spring-form pans.
- Automatic bread makers – *have your Cuisinart call my convection oven and we'll set something up.*
- Pastel bath towels.

1990-1995

- Four-bin recycling centers – *you're consuming less now but recycling it more.*
- Carpet steam cleaners.
- Coffee-table books about the rain forest – *to display next to the crystal geode.*
- Bagel and hand-sliced bread toasters – *when homemade bread is what you can afford.*
- Electric knife sharpeners – *gotta maintain instead of reacquire.*
- Jewel-tone bath towels.

Little White (Lace) Lies

*I*t's not nice to admit this, but people do lie at weddings. Not the sort of lies that make weddings necessary, like "Trust me...," but the sort of fibs that no one believes but everyone uses in the interest of social harmony.

These are not lies – they are shared fantasies, mutually agreed upon, and refusing to participate in them makes you seem a little cantankerous. Besides, who hasn't oozed his or her way out of a tight spot with one of these little gems?

Little Wedding Lies:
1. "You can wear it again."
2. "Your father and I are so happy for you, dear."
3. "My fiancé has been so helpful! He's been involved with every step of the preparations for this wedding!"
4. "I don't really want my wedding to be showy and ostentatious."
5. "This is my daughter's wedding. I won't interfere no matter what she decides to do!"
6. "The best wedding present you could give us would be just to have you at our wedding!"
7. "I'd love it if you'd just call me 'Mom' from now on."
8. "It certainly has been fun meeting all our new in-laws."
9. "Thanks for inviting me to your wedding! It was so *unique*."
10. "What a sweet idea to keep on wearing white at all your weddings, dear."

Thank you for your gift

AND A HEARTY, GENERIC "THANK YOU" TO ALL WHO ATTENDED

It's important to send thank-you notes promptly so people will send you another wedding gift when you get married again. An insincere little written note is customary, although many busy brides like to give a blanket notification of all the loot.

While some purists may blanch at the thought of a picture thank-you note, you should know that it is proper etiquette if the present looks like it was won on the State Fair midway.

"You Can Wear It Again": Recycling Bridesmaid's Gowns

Men and women have a lot of the same problems. Women have to spend a couple hundred dollars buying a bridesmaid's gown. Men spend a couple hundred dollars on a set of radial snow tires. It's a big problem – gowns and radials. What do you do with them after you've used them once?

Where to Wear a Used Bridesmaid's Gown:

1. A bridesmaid's gown would be stunning if you were asked to emcee a "Miss Little Queen Beauty Pageant" for preschoolers.
2. If a member of your family is ever up for sainthood, wear your gown to the canonization proceedings.
3. Wear your bridesmaid's gown if you are ever invited back to formally open the senior prom at your old high school.
4. Parades always need beautiful women in formal gowns, particularly if you don't mind riding on the Miss Turkey Packers float.
5. If you ever have a chance to meet with royalty, your gown will allow you to look at least as stylish as Princess Anne.
6. Since formal picnics are favored by the landed gentry of Britain, it's only a matter of time until the rage for them hits the States. You'll be able to attend in your bridesmaid's gown.
7. If you are a "full-figured" woman, you might be able to sell your gown to a cross-dresser, depending on how campy the wedding was.
8. Start a Former Bridesmaids, Homecoming Queens and Parade Float Attendants Club. Wear your gowns to meetings and go out to dinner. You're certain to attract attention as you enter the restaurant.
9. Cut the gowns into strips and weave them into a powerful tapestry that indicts patriarchal society for using, abusing and discarding the eternal feminine principle, or something.
10. You can fashionably attend funerals in your gown because bridesmaid's gowns are specifically designed to not to draw attention away from the guest of honor.

Term Limits of Endearment

Now that you're well and truly married, you'll have to think up sweet things to call each other for the rest of your life. Best place to find nicknames that are totally embarrassingly is the Valentine's Day personal ads in the newspaper.

Where else would you find monikers like Snookums, Smoochie or Sugar Bugar Bear? Can anyone be so helplessly in love as to enjoy being called Hookie-Hoo, Big Daddy or Momfat? Do little girls dream of marrying Rambo, Horno Borno or Redneck? Do young men look forward to a meaningful relationship with Princess, Turtle Toes or My Lovely Drippy? Yes sir, she's my Baby Cakes, Baby Doll, Babes, Babykins and/or Bambino!

How do you introduce someone? "Mother, I'd like you to meet Captain Naked...." What about, "Pumkin Face used to date Buddah Belly but now is seeing Banana Butt instead?" Do you want your grandchildren to find a trove of ancient letters, tied with a velvet ribbon, starting, "Dearest Bunny Foo Foo," and signed "Your Psycho Love?"

Will self-help groups emerge to raise the esteem of people nicknamed Bubblebutt, Booger Doo, Varicose, Dorky or Geek? And what shall we do with those with positive self-images, like Boobs, Jiggles, Cheeks, Italian Stud, Goddess of Love or Your Little Rosebutton?

I know that love is sweet, but do we need Honey Bear, Honey Boy, Honey Bunches, Honey Melon, Honey Crunch and Honeysuckler? Or Sugar Pie, Sugar Bush, Sugar Bear and Sugums? And what's with the bear metaphor? Cuddle Bear, meet Pooh Bear, Sugar Bear and Teddy Bear. At least you know what Barely Bare is aiming at.

Some names stand alone. Some beg to be seen as a couple. Imagine the dynamics between Goddess and Scruffy Puppy, My Flower and Your Thorn, or Barbarian and Kitten. While some names aren't paired in the personals, perhaps they should be, like Cowboy Man and Howdy Buckarette, Auntie Cookie and Stud Muffin or Hell on Wheels and Trouble. Would Big Dumb Bird love Feathers more than Silly Goose? Will Snugglebunny find happiness with Thumper? Will the Walleye King find his Little Guppy? We seem to spend a lot of time dating outside our species, considering the personals signed by Beast, Weasel, Wolfie, Beef, Wombat, Hamster, Love Bug, Horse and, touchingly, Your Woof.

Some nicknames are so cute they can make you car-sick. Pooky, Punkanoodle, Schmookums and Honey Bunny Boo Boo come immediately to mind. I guess the bottom line is that we'd rather be called Boobala than not called at all. But could you just not do it in public?

MAKING THE MOST OF YOUR HONEYMOON

The trick to a successful honeymoon is to pick a place that's warm but not so hot that you can't have sex if the air-conditioning breaks down.

Honeymoons used to be the time when two virgins first had sex – a time we now call junior high. Nowadays, a honeymoon is primarily a chance to have sex in an exotic location.

Some people spend their honeymoons at a resort where activities are scheduled every fifteen minutes, because they're afraid they won't be able to think of anything to do with their new spouses. Other honeymooning couples come up only for air or lunch, wisely refusing to return home till their Visa cards are maxed out.

You can always identify a couple on their honeymoon, because it is the only time in their lives that they both have new luggage.

Afterwards:
The Honeymoon, Kids and the Rest of Your Life

*P*eople always ask, "Is there life after marriage?" I'm here to tell you that there's more life after marriage than before! A wedding is a rite of passage, but too many brides focus on the *rite* and forget that *passage* means that you're going into something a whole lot more fun than before.

First comes the honeymoon – the only time in your life you can make love in a heart-shaped bed without feeling like a total nincompoop. After the honeymoon, you and your friends can stretch out the wedding and honeymoon debriefings for a good four months. Six months, if you're properly disorganized.

But then it's over, and you've got to get a life. You're not the Princess Bride any more – you're just another married person. Salespeople are only interested in your credit balance and relatives get a little snappish if they haven't gotten their thank-you notes within a year. In short, people no longer treat you as if you're made of porcelain.

This is when a lot of women decide to have a baby. It's another traditional woman's category that involves a lot of fuss and flutter from other women. Everybody wants to talk to you about it, friends host more showers, and strangers smile at you on the streets. It's not that hard to do, and the preparations are rather pleasant. The downside is that giving birth, like suicide, is irrevocable.

After that, life is pretty much downhill. Before long, your gums start to bleed, popular music begins to sound repetitious and your friends gossip more about their surgeries than about each other's sex lives.

This is when you start to plan for *your* daughter's wedding!

Top Honeymoon Tips

*G*oing on a honeymoon is like flying around the world in one week. The experience can be exhilarating, but the jet lag will kill you.

For some folks, it's the only big vacation they'll take on their own, between going with their parents and going with their kids. For others, it's a good chance to get away and write their thank-you notes. Whatever your expectations of your honeymoon, here are some helpful hints:

- Use the special time of your honeymoon to learn all sorts of little things about each other. Like allergies. If you're unaware that your beloved has hay fever, you probably don't realize that bringing your wedding corsage, boutonniere or bouquet into the honeymoon suite and leaving it on the air-conditioning register, where the pollen can blow all over the room, will take your beloved off the romantic fast-track faster than you can say "Gesundheit!"

- Take along a camera with lots of film. You will never look as good as you do on your honeymoon, and you will certainly never both have new wardrobes at the same time again. These pictures will be a great comfort to you later in life, when you can use them to prove to your children that you really were young once, and reasonably good looking, even if you *did* wear weird clothes.

- Don't avoid big tourist attractions just because they're crowded. They're crowded because there's something there to see or do. Crowds validate our experience and let us know that we've seen something beautiful because the place is full of other people looking and saying, "Hey, this is great, you know!"

- You say you want to be alone with your beloved, but think for a second. If you really *are* alone, no one will be able to see and admire your expensive clothes and your plastic luggage with designer initials on it.

- Bags do get lost by airlines, so always carry a toothbrush, your birth control, and some sun block in your purse or pocket. You cannot have a peak sexual experience with a full body sunburn. A honeymoon is a great time to lie in bed whimpering, but not because you forgot the sun block.

- Be aware of a sexual danger no one talks about: the post-coital honeymoon munchies! The reality of animal needs is this: The bride has been on a diet for a couple of months; she has nibbled only ever so daintily at the reception; she's just had a good workout; and room service closes at 11:00 P.M. The most important thing that mothers fail to tell their daughters about their wedding night is to pack a lunch.

Sleeping Together

One of the greatest joys of being married is sleeping with someone every night. That means that by the time you reach your fiftieth wedding anniversary, you will have slept together more than 18,000 times, with time off for bad colds, business trips and those nights you'd rather sleep on the couch than be anywhere near the love of your life.

"Ah ha!" you cry: "You are out of touch with Today's Modern Youth, for we have lived together for years and already *know* all about sleeping with someone!" But Today's Modern Unmarried Youth have no idea how different sleeping together after marriage can be. For one thing, after you're married you can tell your mother the details of what it's like to sleep with your lover and she can't say a thing.

The first year of a marriage is a period of adjustment, during which you have to reconcile your perfectly reasonable demands with the irrational behavior of a maniac. Or so it seems at 3 A.M., an hour at which misunderstandings can arise out of the semiconscious, the unconscious or even the anticonscious behaviors that characterize sleep.

People *do* talk in their sleep. They also argue, shadowbox, jog and occasionally sing snatches of operatic arias. To help you learn about these pitfalls before your marriage ends up at the sleep-disorders clinic, the divorce court or both, here's a quick overview of common sleep issues.

The Unconscious Response

Talking in your sleep is bad enough, but at least the impulse comes from inside you. Things really get crazy when your subconscious has to respond to an outside stimulus. We have vivid imaginations when we're asleep, and feelings aren't the only thing that can get hurt here. For example, your husband isn't being aggressive when he flops his hand onto your face in the middle of the night. But if you're dreaming about mutant seaweed slime monsters when that clammy hand cuts you off in midsnore, you'll respond heroically. You'll wrestle with that mutant until you're safe or until you've broken a finger.

The problem is that your husband is sound asleep too. Suddenly it's *his* turn to respond to an outside stimulus. God knows what he's been dreaming about, but whatever it was, it's trying to break his fingers. Things usually don't get this dramatic, but you'll soon learn where your sweetie doesn't want to be touched in the middle of the night. If he snaps, snarls or barks – back off. It's nothing personal – he hasn't the slightest idea of who you are. Besides, he might be dreaming about mutant seaweed slime monsters.

Sleeping with an Animal

"Sleeping with an animal" is not a cute way of saying you've got a wild sex life ahead of you. It just means you've wandered into a "Love me, love my dog," or more likely, "Love me, worship my cat" type relationship. Sleeping with animals raises the sort of profound questions human beings have been asking ever since prehistory. Questions like: "What exactly *are* the territorial needs of cats and what will they do to defend them?" to say nothing of "Who said my pillow was part of their territory?"

But as the psychologists say, the real issue is not with the cat or dog. The deeper problem is that you've got unresolved issues with your parents, particularly if your parents were in the habit of sleeping on the foot of your bed. So work this out with your spouse before you go to bed. Just remember that most people interpret any rejection of their cats as a personal attack on them. Good luck.

Snore Is Less

It's horrifying how a person who appears so kind, considerate and caring during the courtship can turn into such a world-class foghorn after the wedding. People are always on their best behavior before they're married: Women don't drape pantyhose all over the bathroom, men don't spit out of car windows, and nobody at all, ever, ever snores.

It isn't the sex that takes getting used to – it's having that paw land in your face at 3 A.M. that will get you every time.

You don't have to suffer in silence while your partner saws wood. The physical-barrier method of snore control is best. Since snoring comes out of the mouth, to stop snoring, stop up the mouth. The perpetrator will probably still be able to breathe through his or her nose, so go ahead – stuff in whatever you can find that will stop that annoying sound – socks, wadded Kleenex, pillows, whatever.

The up side is that this is a proven, certain method of stopping snoring. The down side is that occasionally manslaughter charges may result.

YOUR CHILDREN FIND YOUR WEDDING ALBUM

Your children know the funniest book in your house is your wedding album. No matter how polite they are, your kids just can't believe that anybody ever wore the clothes you were married in, appeared in public in the hairdo that your spouse so loved, or just generally looked so doofy.

This is because weddings are about our deepest, most cherished beliefs and feelings, and nothing ages as badly as the emotional excesses of a generation.

For example, let's say that you wrote your own vows and had someone read this really right-on poem you found in the liner notes of your favorite album. Worse yet, you were probably so moved by all this that you had a calligrapher write it down on fake parchment.

Unless your kids are walking around wearing beaded bellbottoms saying "Groovy," you've got a problem here. How can you expect a generation raised on compact discs (featuring artwork too small to stare at for hours) to understand the cultural and literary significance of liner notes to their parent's generation?

The CD generation will fail to understand the album crowd just as surely as the hi-fi generation misunderstood the 78 RPM'ers, who, in turn, didn't have a clue about their wax-cylinder forebears. And your kids never *will* understand until some new technology makes their own music library obsolete.

The best revenge is to wait until you can show *their* wedding album to *their* kids!

Swell Stuff Your Spouse Has Been Hiding from You

A lot of men are afraid that if they get in touch with their feminine side, they'll start retaining water. A lot of women think that if they ever get assertive, they'll develop a beer belly. Marriage is the process of breaking down these separatist notions and learning that your way of doing things may not be divinely ordained after all.

Men and women differ not only in the way they approach problems but in the tools they bring along. It takes a few years of marriage to discover what the opposite sex has been hiding from you all this time.

Neat Things Women Have That They Don't Share With Men

Pantyhose: Oh, sure, I've heard all about their drawbacks: that they're hot in the summer and not that warm in the winter, that they can pop and give thigh burns that never heal and that by the end of a day they ride lower on your butt than a stripper's G-string. But the genius of pantyhose is that, unlike men's socks, once you find *one*, you've got a *pair*. There's no fumbling in the morning half-light trying to match two socks for length, texture and color. What's more, you can throw them away with a clear conscience at the first sign of a hole.

Emery boards: Men prefer clippers because they're higher-tech than an emery board, but about fifteen years into their marriage, men finally realize that nail files work better on a dinged fingernail that's bound to rip off right down to the cuticle. Until they figure this out, men instinctively haul out the scissors on their Swiss Army knife and hack that nail right down to the bloody stump. And women wonder where military thinking comes from!

Freedom from neckties: Some men think neckties are phallic symbols, but then, some men think anything that's longer than it's wide is a phallic symbol. My theory is that ties are symbolic only if your privates are colored a bright paisley or can be tied in any of three fashionable knots. Neckties are sort of like pantyhose for the neck. They're constricting, they're hot, they chafe and they can look like hell without your knowing it. The only thing they're better than is bow ties.

Forks: Women have forks. Men don't. That's why traditional male cuisine is eaten with fingers (burgers, pizza, hot dogs), chopsticks (take-out Chinese) or flimsy plastic forks that come with the meal (Kentucky Fried Chicken). Forks disappear on men because men eat anywhere there's a flat surface to set a plate on. When they do take their plate back to the sink, the fork usually gets left behind. That's why you never want to walk barefooted in a bachelor's apartment.

Fun Stuff Men Have That Women Don't Have a Clue About

Pants: Skirts are a joke that men played on women that women never got. There's enough cold wind whistling around and up a skirt to set off wind chimes. With pants, you never have to worry about keeping your knees together, you never have to tug your trousers before you sit down (although you can get a nasty case of the snuggies), and you're warm. Plus you get to wear belts with big gaudy buckles.

Meeting modifiers: Life is a series of excruciatingly dull meetings, and the secret is to find something to occupy your mind. Women don't know this, so they fold their hands atop the table and try to look caring and involved. Men stare at their laps, or at least they seem to. What they're really doing is folding and unfolding their Swiss Army knives or playing cribbage on their wingtips. That's what those little holes are for – to keep you from going insane while your boss reinvents the wheel.

The Triple T: Men live by the Triple T: toys, tools and testosterone. On occasion, women can find the testosterone part pretty exhilarating, but they never really warm up to the toys and tools. Some women claim that toys are just a man's way of being aggressive even when his body is inert, as when a couch potato sends a little radio-controlled dune buggy banging around the living room knocking over lamps. While women are hell-bent on growing up, men refuse to go anywhere the problems are so complex that Black and Decker doesn't make a tool to fix them.

Design-free homes: Men and women experience space differently, so it stands to reason that they would furnish a home differently. Women decorate walls; men decorate by filling floor space. Men decorate with technology: Put a CD player with six-foot speakers, a large-screen TV, a three-foot aquarium and two metal folding chairs in the middle of a room and a man would consider the room finished. A woman, on the other hand, would hang a floral print on the wall of an empty room and invite friends over. As soon as a woman gets enough money, she has someone redesign her home till it looks like somebody else lives there. Male decor is individualistic, although a lot of male furniture looks like it came out of a customized van.

Duct tape: The unifying element in a many a man's life is duct tape because it can hold together anything except a bad marriage. Like most men, duct tape isn't much to look at, but it's strong and dependable. When you think about it, it's surprising that country-western singers don't do tear-jerker songs about duct tape.

Celebrating Your Anniversary in the 21st Century

*F*reud used to ponder: "What do women want?" If he had ever thought to ask Mrs. Freud, she would have said, "I want you to remember our anniversary, dumkopf!"

All women remember every anniversary, and no man ever remembers any. Yes, that is a sexist, anecdotal and unscientific statement, and I defy anyone to disprove it. Oh, sure, some men are pretty good about remembering their anniversaries, but then some guys floss after every meal.

On the other hand, some people celebrate their anniversary every chance they get. If they were married on the seventh of September, they celebrate the seventh of everything: Seventh Street, seven P.M., October seventh, November seventh and so on. That sort of marriage will wear out before it rusts out.

Men don't like to admit it, but they're intimidated by the rituals of anniversaries. They can never remember whether the sixth anniversary is supposed to be the Woolen Wedding Anniversary or the Wooden Wedding Anniversary. And they know their wives have those little cards Hallmark hands out that tell which anniversary is which. They know they'll be graded and if they get it wrong it will go on their permanent records, so they decide, what the hell, I'll just pretend I forgot again.

We need some updated anniversary gifts that reflect the economic realities and interests of today's couples. Here are some suggestions.

New Anniversary Gifts

1: **The Coupon Anniversary.** A coupon wallet to hold grocery-store coupons and entertainment-coupon books would be appreciated.

2: **The Cordless Anniversary.** Keep in touch with cordless telephones, vibrators, shavers, screwdrivers and electronic gadgets of all kinds.

3: **The Cookbook Anniversary.** Time to start collecting exotic cookbooks you'll never use for the entertaining you'll never do.

4: **The Undie Anniversary.** Special underwear for special nights, in leather, lace and silky see-through.

5: **The Renewal Anniversary.** Prove your love by renewing your vows and prove your fidelity by renewing your blood tests on your fifth!

6: **The Remote-Control Anniversary.** Fast-forward into fun with remote controls for your VCR, TV and CD, and don't overlook RC model airplanes, tiny race cars and little-bitty boats.

7: **The Recycling Anniversary.** Trash compactors and newspaper bundling racks may not be romantic, but you'll know that you're doing the *right thing.*

8: **The High-Tech Anniversary.** High-tech kitchen gadgets can make cooking a techno-task fit for a man. In other words, get off your butt and help!

9: **The Health-Club Anniversary.** Treat each other to a health club membership – to get back into the shape you're not *really* out of.

10: **The Hot Band Anniversary.** Hire a hot band and a hot tub for a hot party celebrating your decade.

15: **The Fix-It-Up Anniversary.** Wouldn't it be nice to do a little remodeling and have a new kitchen, a new patio or maybe just a new furnace?

20: **The Clean-It-Up Anniversary.** Carpet Sweepers and Shop-Vacs have saved many a marriage, if only because you can't argue with the vacuum on.

25: **The Get-Away-from-It Anniversary.** You waited till the kids were grown to take that exotic vacation, and now you can't remember where you wanted to go.

30: **The Internal Combustion Anniversary.** Now you can afford that *big* petrochemical toy you've always wanted – the big honker car or the motor home long enough to have its own zip code. You're free to go anywhere you can find an RV hookup.

35: **The Condo Anniversary.** Sell the snow shovel; buy a condo in Florida. Now you need mildew-resistant furniture, plastic beach sandals and paper plates that you can take to the pool.

40: **The His & Hers Anniversary.** You're retired and you're a 24-hour-a-day couple again! You need his and her bicycles to get out of each other's hair and his and her Barcaloungers when you come back!

45: **The Bragging Anniversary.** Framed graduation pictures of all the grandchildren and newspaper clippings of your kids (to show everyone) make wonderful gifts.

50: **The Unlikely Anniversary.** Used to be called the Golden Anniversary, but even with today's longevity, let's get real about marriage statistics.

75: **The Unheard-of Anniversary.**

EXCHANGING THE AISLE FOR THE ISLE

A wedding is supposed to be a joyous occasion. Sometimes the best way to make sure that it is joyous is to leave the relatives far behind and announce your nuptials by shortwave radio.

Getting married on a tropical island (or at the airport on the way to one) may be the answer to your nuptial nightmares. Wouldn't it be more romantic to swim with the dolphins than do the hora with your Aunt Esther? Dealing with customs officials in a foreign language certainly would be less stressful than coping with a caterer who has ten fewer plates than you have guests. Wouldn't listening to marimba music be more relaxing than hearing "Feelings" played for the tenth time?

And you *know* that sunbathing on a private, palm-fringed nude beach certainly would be sexier than sitting through a lingerie-and-marital-aids shower with your elderly aunts.

We're Not Going to the Chapel: Nontraditional Weddings

Not every woman lusts after a wedding that would pauperize the British royal family. Some women just want to have fun.

Some women did the Big White Dress routine with the Really Wrong Groom and don't want to draw that much attention to their second chance. Some aren't involved in any particular church, or are marrying someone their church doesn't like.

So instead of dropping another $20,000 on a party approved by Martha Stewart, they opt for creativity and imagination and get married where they feel comfortable.

Wedding ceremonies have been held at the amusement park where the couple first dated, at the couple's favorite bar and at a liquor store. They have been held at a dinner theater, at a movie theater and at a movie premiere. Folks have gotten married at the complaint office, at a bookstore, at a bowling alley, at a polka ballroom, at a bank, at a horse-racing track and at the Ramsey County Adult Detention Center, a spot recommended by one municipal judge because it has "such a beautiful view of the city and the [Mississippi] river."

People have gotten married in a hospital, a nursing home, a night club, an ice palace, a McDonald's parking lot, caves and city, state and national parks. One fireman got married in a burning house to a bride with a fire extinguisher.

Couples have taken the plunge from a fishing boat and an ice fishing house. Marriages have occurred during earthquakes, during a cross-country bike trip, during halftime at a football game and during tailgate parties. People even have been married during regular Sunday services.

Weddings have been performed under waterfalls and jumping off bridges, attached to a bungee cord. A divorced couple was remarried on the walkway over a dam to show that everything that had gone on before was water over the dam. The knot has been tied on the golf course, on the phone, on a hang glider, on skis, on water skis, on the dance floor and on a hockey rink with a faceoff between the bride's team and the groom's team after the nuptials.

The bride and groom have arrived at their weddings in everything from manure spreaders to horses (perhaps that's redundant) and left on garbage trucks, snowmobiles and motorcycles built for two. It just takes planning. If you're going to speed away on a motorcycle, make sure your wedding dress has a tear-away skirt so you can exit in a spray of stones without getting your train caught in the spokes.

Second Weddings: "Encore" or Just Strike Two?

*S*econd weddings are now called "encore" weddings because nobody would dream of spending another ten to thirty grand on a "second chance" party. But at an "encore" wedding, the bride can have it all. Again. The big honker white dress, the nine bridesmaids (who might be getting a little testy by now), and a satin train long enough to sweep up oil slicks.

Nobody in their right mind still thinks that only virgins qualify for white dresses, but some people still get smart-mouthed about the second $3,000 gown you've bought in five years. So how do you justify another huge, ego-stroking blowout? (Obviously, you can't call it "going back for seconds.") You just act as if it were your first wedding, because while it isn't the first time you've been married, it *is* the first time you've been married to this person. (By this logic, one hundred bridesmaids can dance on the head of a pin.)

"Encore" has such a nice sound. All that applause, the public acclaim to see you play the scene again (albeit with a different cast) the flowers thrown over the footlights – and the silencing of the critics. It's so much more dignified for the oft-wedded than standing at the altar shouting "NEXT!..."

If anything is traditional about American weddings, "encore" weddings embody it. There is no historical or religious precedent for such a celebration – we have willed it into being. We do it to please ourselves and to give honor to a fresh start in life. We blend cultures, customs, religions and beliefs together and gulp it whole.

Sure sounds American to me.

From Polygyny to Pantagamy: Marriage Alternatives You'd Rather Not Hear about

There's a lot of talk about family values nowadays, but before you start agreeing, you'd better be certain what kind of family they're talking about. Americans assume that every culture throughout history has practiced our form of monogamy (one husband, one wife, 2.5 children and a thirty-year mortgage).

But whenever sex is involved, people are endlessly inventive, and there's no mathematical combination that hasn't been tried somewhere, sometime: bigamy (two spouses), trigamy (three spouses) and so on to polygamy (lots and lots).

Technically, a man with more than two women in his life is engaging in polygyny, whereas a woman with more than one male is dabbling in polyandry. Digamists are folks who have legally remarried after the death of their first spouse, although a disonogamist probably has a trophy wife, since he's married to someone of markedly different age. He probably fled what he thought was heterogamosis, or marriage between people who are distinctly unsuitable for each other. Serial monogamy occurs when you're faithful to one spouse at a time, but the clock is running.

We talk about marrying into a family, but in ancient times that wasn't just a figure of speech. In leviration, a man was required to marry his brother's widow, but in sororate, a man had to marry his wife's sister if his wife died.

Brothers must have gotten along better in ancient times, because they were continually getting involved in group scenes that today would end in bloodshed or at least headlines in the *National Enquirer*. In adelphogamy, some brothers have a common wife or wives. The ancient Hawaiians were said to have messed with punalua, a group marriage in which several brothers marry several sisters, and nobody could remember who was supposed to take out the trash. Finally we get to pantagamy, a community marriage where every woman is married to every man.

If this all sounds tribal, you're right. Marriages have always been viewed in terms of whether they reinforce or transcend boundaries. Mésalliance is a marriage to someone of markedly lower social status; miscegenation, marriage between races; and exogamy, marriage outside one's own tribe, group, class or country club. Royal families have always preferred endogamy, or inbreeding, which after a few generations often results in big ears, weak chins and peasant revolts.

These marriages are complex enough. There's no telling what happened at the weddings. I'm not even certain I want to know.

Alternative Weddings: Not Just for Hippies Anymore

Nontraditional weddings are thriving and their quirky vitality embodies the best of American weddings. They're cussedly independent, self-reliant and nearly spontaneous. They owe more to imagination than to tradition. Pomposity is held to a minimum, if not openly lampooned, although the level of sentimentality can sometimes approach toxic levels.

Americans want to get married in the darnedest places, as nearly any mother of the bride can tell you. In what other country would someone propose to be married on Halloween in a cemetery with the bride wearing a black dress and skeleton earrings under a black veil, while the groom carried a plastic skull scepter and wore a black tux and a T-shirt with a skull printed on it?

Let's do a quick processional through some amazing weddings.

Nudist Weddings
American nudists are ordinary folks with profoundly conventional morality who do one exceptional thing. They run around "fabric free" as often as possible. They have succeeded among themselves in separating nudity from shame and, so far as I can tell, from inter-mural sex.

Nudists are forever talking about how positive and healthful their lifestyle is and how it helps keep families together. Their literature is full of pink people of all ages looking no more awkward than people normally do in photographs. The only common element seems to be that they're all buck-assed naked.

Nudists get married like everybody else, although the ceremonies are seldom covered in the society pages. How can you talk about the bride's attire if all she wore was a number 15 sunblock?

Like most of nudist life, nudist weddings are a little shy about the outside fabric world which tends to see nudity as some sort of sexual abandon. Like gay weddings, nude weddings have particular problems with which relatives to invite. There's the problem of free-floating disapproval, plus the problem of the dress code, which becomes a matter of the liveliest interest to outsiders. You probably haven't been, and never will be, invited to a true nudist wedding, so relax. Besides, you're probably a lot more interested in seeing theirs than they are in seeing yours.

Scuba Weddings
Scuba diving is a perfect metaphor for marriage: The two of you are in an alien environment where you can't survive without the help of your buddy.

The first recorded underwater wedding was in June 1935, when 73-year-old John C. Benson and his unnamed bride, dressed in leaky diving gear, attached to an air pump that jammed and connected to each other and the minister by telephone wires, were married eight feet below Puget Sound.

Scuba engagements are more common than scuba weddings, perhaps because there are so few mothers of brides who dive. One fellow proposed to his sweetie by slipping a ring into her diving vest and popping the question by writing on his underwater tablet. She accepted – fortunately for him, because the rest of the divers had decorated the dive boat with balloons to celebrate. "I think I would just have stayed underwater if she had said no," he admitted.

Greg Lashbrook and Kathy Johnson, the authors of *A Diving and Snorkeling Guide to the Great Lakes*, met in a scuba class, became engaged underwater and were married at thirty feet. Greg had always said that if he ever got married again, it would be underwater. Kathy thought that was "pretty weird" and her parents thought it was entirely crazy.

Crazy, but not impossible. Kathy and Greg worked for a commercial diving company and had access to a communications system that enabled them to speak and be heard underwater. Underwater ceremonies usually aren't fully legal because you can't speak. You have to get married topside so the officiant can hear, then you can dive and exchange your "I do's" written on tablets. But this would be a living, speaking, bubbling, legal wedding!

They netted a diving judge and eighteen divers to witness the ceremony. The bride wore a lace veil and a white wet suit trimmed with lace, and the groom wore a wet suit that resembled a tuxedo. The bride's father swam her away. The nondiving guests (along with eight reporters) stayed on six boats and watched the ceremony on video monitors.

Why did Kathy and Greg want a scuba wedding? For the best of reasons: "We feel most comfortable underwater."

Parachute Weddings

Some people shy away from parachute weddings because they feel that making a promise "till death do us part" and then jumping out of an airplane is tempting fate.

If you're intent on a skydiving wedding, please do it inside the plane before you jump out. The speediest civil ceremony takes at least five minutes, but freefall only averages forty-five seconds. With that kind of time frame, you can pretty much rule out a high mass in formation.

If you insist on getting high at your wedding, consider a hot-air balloon. For one thing, it's easier to find a priest, minister or judge who will go up in a balloon than to find one who will go down in a parachute.

Minnesota Judge Howard Albertson has done several balloon weddings, and he's learned the importance of watching the wind. When Kristi Larson and Jeff Wessel got married at 1,500 feet, the wind swung around and the balloon began to drift east over the St. Croix River into Wisconsin.

Albertson hurried through the rest of the ceremony and had the couple safely and legally married before they drifted out of his jurisdiction.

Las Vegas Weddings

Las Vegas is a desert resort where nobody wears shorts and nobody comes home with a tan. Where Wayne Newton is such an important guy that there's a street named after him; where you're just a hop, skip and a half-life from the army's nuclear test range; and where the major tourist attractions are the Liberace Museum, a marshmallow factory and the Hoover dam.

Las Vegas is a permanent convention of compulsives, and there isn't an itch that they aren't prepared to scratch. Gambling? That's what they're there for! Drinking? They're watering the desert with the stuff! Girls (and/or boys)? Prostitution is legal in Nevada! Shopping? The high-ticket malls have arrived! Overeating? Only $1.99 for the All-U-Can-Eat Buffet! Stand on a street corner in Las Vegas and shout, "Just say no," and people will laugh so hard that their eyes will clear up.

On top of all that, you can even get married in Las Vegas. Boy, can you get married! Twenty-four hours a day, ten minutes a pop, flowers and champagne extra, drive-up, walk-through, cruising the strip in a motor-home chapel, or if you're into convenience, they'll come to your room and hitch you there.

Charlotte Richards is the Wedding Queen of the West (and closing in on being the Wedding Queen of

The Wedding Queen of the West calls from her Drive-thru wedding window in Las Vegas, Nevada.

the World), from the "I Wed U" license plates on her pale-yellow Cadillac to the oversized heart pendant she wears at her throat.

She's married more than half a million people, including Joan Collins, Frank Sinatra, Mickey Rooney (a couple of times, actually) and Michael Jordan.

Charlotte opened the first drive-thru wedding window on Valentine's Day and had them lined up down the block. She has four chapels, fifteen limos, her own flower shop, a staff of fifty people and a wedding van that can take the couple and their friends wherever they want to go to get married.

Charlotte gets excited talking about all the couples she's married. Like the couple that met and was married within the hour. Another couple met at a new millionaire's banquet – they had both won a state lottery and needed a partner who would understand the burden of sudden wealth. Or the couple who had been living together for forty years and decided to make it legal before they reached retirement age. It's one thing to upset your parents, but nobody messes with the Social Security people!

Clown Weddings

Who doesn't like clowns, the mimes of the trailer-park set? Who doesn't love laughing at a stylized hobo as he beats another stylized hobo with a stylized bat?

Clowns proudly claim that clowning dates back to the Italian Renaissance street theater of *commedia del arte*. But *commedia* picked on the fools of the world – vainglorious generals, greedy merchants, idiotic doctors and star-eyed lovers – not just bums. Wouldn't it be fun to go to a circus and see clowns portraying White House aides, airline executives and sullen, millionaire athletes?

Clowns fall in love like everybody else and when they do, the temptation to get married in costume is nearly irresistible, if only because the *National Enquirer* will cover the wedding, and make you a national celebrity. Clowns can do fun stuff at the ceremony, like having a squirting Unity candle or a hand buzzer for the receiving line. Someone with a clown ministry can do balloon tricks to illustrate scripture lessons, and the mother of the bride can wear a pot of flowers on her head.

Understandably, this sort of thing isn't for everyone, and a clown's wedding guest list may have to be skewed toward the grade-school set. But if you don't mind having a Ninja Turtle wedding cake, it's a great idea.

Pet Weddings

Lots of people will marry pets for you, and it's safe to say that none of them think a wedding for a beast is either funny or vaguely blasphemous. One woman got into the business for the most moral of reasons. Her six-year-old granddaughter worried that animals were having babies without benefit of the clergy. So Dawn Rogers sent away for a mail-order theological degree from the Universal Life Church and has married dozens of animals since. A responsible chaplain, Rogers refuses to bless the union of animals already in heat and, to avoid miscegenation, will marry only within the same

species. There's no way to know what she would say about the Los Angeles secretary who invited twenty close, personal friends to share in her joy as she married a fifty-pound rock.

Horseback Weddings

Weddings on horseback have become increasingly popular with the sort of people who go to dude ranches and pay someone to let them stare at cows.

One "minister" in Michigan performs horseback weddings in the Detroit parks, as well as advertising in nudist magazines for "fabric free" weddings. I have no idea whether she also does nude horseback weddings in the Detroit parks, although the number of things you could chafe sitting buck-naked in a saddle is truly awesome.

But what about the people for whom a horse isn't a mere affectation – real ranchers, not urban cowboys? Where do rodeo stars get married? Not on their horse, you can bet your spurs. Dondee Krolikowski of Interior, So.Dak., has a closet full of big belt buckles she's won in rodeos. Watching her ride is like watching water flow downhill. Her whole family rides, except for the dog. So did she go to a Detroit park and get married on horseback?

Not on your life! "You'd get your wedding gown just filthy on horseback!" she hoots. All she wanted when she got married was to get into a beautiful dress and have a big party for her friends and family.

Cowboys are considered the world's most romantic men (at least by cowgirls). One Wyoming woman recalls going to a dance filled with tall,

Would a rodeo star be a bride on horseback? Not on your life!

gorgeous men with big hats, where a little fellow caught her eye. They struck up a conversation and in due time drove out to the rodeo grounds to sit on the hood of her car as they watched the sun come up over the Yellowstone River.

Now *that's* cowboy romance! Detroit parks, my chapped elbow.

Grocery Store Weddings

When you're in love, an aisle is an aisle, whether it's lined with Campbell's soup or dewy-eyed relatives. This is particularly true if you met and fell in love in a grocery store. David Decker and Jenelu Harfiel worked at the Country Market in Elk River, Minn., and fell in love over ice-cream samples. They were married on an altar area made of Coca-Cola twelve-packs by a minister who used to work in the produce department.

Renaissance Fair Weddings

There's something about the Middle Ages that unhinges people's minds and lets in all sorts of romantic bombast about knights in iron knickers and distressed-out damsels.

Since most of us haven't the foggiest idea what life was like in the Middle Ages (which we think covers everything from the fall of the Roman Empire to the invention of the steam engine), we project our own psychological needs onto the time. Americans see knights as proto-cowboys: isolated loners outside the rule of law who pass their time fighting dragons – an oddly phallic obsession.

Chivalry is big business nowdays. In Florida, you can eat Medieval-style southern fried chicken off pewter plates while you watch knights jousting. In Las Vegas, the newest, biggest hotel is called the Excalibur and they dress the help in "medieval-flair" costumes. "Flair" means "sort of," like "para-," as in "para-legal," or "para-medic." When you call the Excalibur, they answer the phone, "Have a Royal Day!" And because it's Las Vegas, you can get married at the Canterbury wedding chapel in medieval costumes (a gown for the woman, a one-size-fits-all Merlin robe for the groom).

Or you can get married at one of the New World's many Renaissance Fairs, as Jean and Steven Brill did. They said they liked the make-believe atmosphere of the Fair (where you are addressed as "M'Lord," or "M'Lady" instead of "Yo...") and they liked being able to bring along Jean's dog.

They asked themselves, is the traditional wedding gown any less of a costume than a Renaissance gown? And are doublets and body tights which totally prevent you from going to the bathroom without hysteria any worse than a tuxedo? Of course not! Jean wore a teal wedding gown fashioned along Renaissance lines. ("Medieval-flair" as they say.) The groom's two daughters were part of the ceremony, as was the dog, who was on a leash made of the same material as the bride's dress. As Jean proudly admitted: "He looked real regal."

Softball Weddings

Many brides have felt like widows during the state basketball tournament, the World Series, the Stanley Cup playoffs or Super Bowl Sunday. So it's nice to report that sometimes the cleats are on the other foot.

Roxanne Palmquist and Mark Hudak had a traditional church wedding planned for August 28, but that was before the Forest Lake, Minn., American Legion slow-pitch softball team won the playoffs and went to the state tournament.

Roxanne was the star center fielder for Forest Lake, and while Mark meant a lot to her, she also knew that an athlete's knees give out on her and there would be no telling whether she would get to the state tournament again.

So they arranged to get married between tournament games. She won the first game against Valnes Well-Drilling of Morris but lost to D&B

Getting married on top of a Mayan pyramid isn't a good idea if you're going to invite a lot of elderly relatives who use walkers.

Freight Sales of Crookston. As soon as that game ended, Roxanne ran for the showers, got out of her cleats and into her wedding dress. Her father escorted her back onto the field, where Mark waited in his tux. They were married at home plate.

Roxanne's team didn't win the title that year, but they did well. Mark also plays softball but his team didn't make it to the playoffs. And who says women never marry beneath themselves?

Mayan Weddings

Thousands of Americans on package tours troop through Chichen Itza, give it a quick once-over and head back to Cancun for some volleyball and a piña colada. Then they go home and tell their friends about how moved they were by their experience with the ancient Mayan (or was it Aztec?) civilization.

Hundreds of others push on to Tulum, the Mayan Miami Beach, a splashy little beachfront property with great cliffs. But darned few North Americans go as far as Sidney Hollander and Cherry Lynette Hamman did.

He was a mathematician obsessed with the Mayan 52-year calendar. She was a graduate student researching the dietary habits of the Maya. They met and fell in love in a dugout canoe on the Pasión river in Guatemala and decided to get married atop a thousand-year-old structure called the Temple of the Seven Dolls. They even reconstructed the ancient Mayan wedding ceremony by digging through museum manuscripts.

The bride carried a spray of pink frangipani and wore an elaborately embroidered *huipil* with copper bells in her hair. The groom wore a traditional *guayabera*, white trousers and a Panama hat. They presented each other with five cacao beans (which represented some serious money to an ancient Mayan), while the wise man from the village of Telchaquillo invoked the gods of Earth, Fire, Water and Air, the local deities of Dzibilchaltún and, just to cover all the bases, a few Catholic saints and the Apostles.

Their reception featured a feast of shredded venison simmered in an underground oven and turkey marinated in chili for three days, wrapped in corn husks and burned black. And *balché*. The ancient Maya considered *balché* the wine of the gods and the Spaniards must have agreed because they not only destroyed the Mayan culture, but banned the growing of *balché* trees. The Conquistadores were the original "Just Say No" crowd. It didn't work back then either and the trees still exist.

After the ceremony, the guests streamed up the steep steps of the pyramid to congratulate the couple. I don't believe I've *ever* seen anybody stream up Mayan steps, although I have seen one or two folks who could honestly be said to be streaming down. You'd be in particular danger of streaming down after a hit or two of *balché*.

Ferris Wheel Weddings
Where would you expect the merry-go-round foreman and a carnival concession-stand worker to get married? On a Ferris wheel decked out with green crepe paper, of course. Micki Seitz and Wayne Kohler sat in the first bucket, with the rest of the wedding party seated around the wheel. But Gertrude Tornbom, the justice of the peace, refused to stand up in a moving Ferris wheel bucket, so they stopped the wheel while she stood on solid ground.

Jail Weddings
Perhaps it's the effect of too much claptrap TV; perhaps it's just a deep-seated masochism; but there's something appealing to a lot of people, particularly women, about convicts. As one person put it, "Everybody looks good when they're in custody."

Who doesn't love a romantic outlaw? Sue Terry of Centralia, Ill., recently announced her engagement to John Wayne Gacy, who is on the Illinois death row for murdering thirty-three men and boys. Standing by her man, Terry (the mother of eight children) dismissed the charges against her fiancé, saying, "I don't believe hardly any of it."

Just because this country is executing people at a record pace doesn't mean we're heartless and unromantic. Florida, one of the nation's leading executioners, recently passed a law allowing death-row inmates to marry.

If you like reading about these nuptials, don't read the society pages. Read the advice columns. A twenty-one-year-old woman with a thirty-two-year-old prison beau felt guilty that he was in prison. After all, it was her former boyfriend who tried to kill them, but her current boyfriend took away the gun and shot an innocent bystander, so now he's in jail and he's all the time calling her and ragging on her and she doesn't know whether she should leave him or stick by his side and can Diane Crowley "please write back quick before I go crazy?" Honey, the mail doesn't travel that fast.

Weddings that Go Wrong

Weddings can go terribly wrong and we're not just talking about a unity candle that won't light. At a wedding in Missouri recently, a woman whom the groom didn't know, but who had a crush on him, stood up and started shooting at the bride and the groom as they knelt at the altar. She missed them, but then shot herself in the head. The wedding resumed an hour later, but the bride's grandmother died of a heart attack at the reception. How are you going to celebrate the anniversary of *that* wedding with any enthusiasm?

One wedding that won't have anniversaries came about because ministers, unlike bars, don't ask for ID. Kathleen Michaels and James Craig of Indiana were going to be married by a Minnesota judge, but arrived after the courthouse had closed for the weekend. Luckily, one of the courthouse janitors just happened to be an ordained Assembly of God minister, so on his lunch break, he married them on the government center steps.

The media had a field day with this romantic story. That was a mistake. The couple should have asked for a private ceremony. Two days later, Mr. & Mrs. Phil Michaels heard the news. First they canceled the missing person's report they had filed on their daughter and then they started annulment proceedings – it seems that Kathleen was only 14, not 18 as she had told the minister/janitor. "For a 14-year-old, she looked 21 at least," the baffled minister recalled.

Nor should we forget the Minnesota couple who chartered a 47-foot boat on Lake Minnetonka for their wedding. When the time came to exchange vows, the bride, groom and the minister stood amidship and everyone else politely moved to the stern of the boat. The boat went nose up and promptly sank. Luckily, no one was hurt.

Judging Weddings

Contrary to popular belief, a wedding performed by a judge is not subject to appeal to the Supreme Court. You're married and that's it. Don't even think about parole.

So who gets married by a judge? Folks of different faiths often find a civil ceremony comforting; older couples who don't want a big Barbie-doll wedding; and a lot of second (and subsequent) marriages.

Judges often are asked to marry people whom

they have sentenced to prison. As Judge Joseph Summers of Ramsey County, Minnesota, sees it, "They call the judge they know." Judges meet lots of colorful people. Judge Patricia Belois of Hennepin County, Minnesota, recalls two young people who wanted to exchange earrings – not rings – during the ceremony. And not just any earrings but the miniature handcuffs that many police officers wear as tie tacks. Unfortunately, the holes in their ears had grown shut, and when they forced the little handcuffs through each other's earlobes, things turned a bit bloody.

Martha Stewart wouldn't have approved.

Cemetery Weddings

In a country where the bombs are smarter than many high school graduates, it shouldn't be surprising that some folks feel right at home with ghoulish weddings. The people at Forest Lawn Cemetery see nothing ghoulish about death. This major Los Angeles tourist attraction was conceived as a place "where lovers new and old shall love to stroll" through grave sections with names like Lullabyland or Slumberland. Forest Lawn's four picturesque churches all are available for weddings, christenings and funerals. Since the cemetery opened its crypt gates to weddings in the early 1920s, more than 60,000 weddings have been held there.

But in Indiana, on All Hallows E'en of 1990, Stephanie Plemmons, 23, was quite literally the bride of Frankenstein. Dressed in white with lightning bolts in her hair, Plemmons married Glen Hettenbach, 42, who was dressed as Frankenstein's monster. The bridesmaids carried orange and black flowers, and the flower girl bedecked the aisle with dead leaves. The bride's two-year-old son came as a green dinosaur. Commenting on her wedding, Plemmons mused, "My friends think I'm crazy, but we're going to have a lot of people talking."

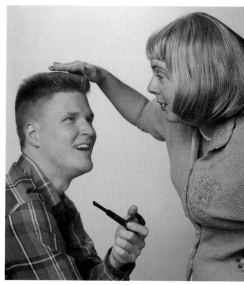

Brides Through the Ages:
A Short Survey of Brides and Their Settings

There isn't much tradition in today's neotraditional weddings because tradition is limited to what actually happened. Fantasy is what we wished had happened, and sentimentality is what we assume our ancestors would have done if they had only had enough money.

"Weddings are returning to tradition!" we are told with sincerity and enthusiasm by the Marital-Industrial Complex. What they mean is that weddings are getting bigger, more fantastic and more sentimental.

Thirty years ago, weddings were a $3 billion a year industry. Today, they're raking in $31 billion a year. Last thing the industry wants is a return to tradition.

Tradition would be having your reception in the church basement. People don't do that anymore because you can't serve booze in a church. Besides, the church basement has been converted into a foodshelf. That reception would be catered by the Ladies Aid Society and you'd take what they made.

Tradition would be a black dress. In frontier America, there was little money to squander on luxuries, and Sunday-go-to-meetin' clothes were black for both men and women. Only the very rich could throw away money on a gown that was worn a single time. It wasn't till after World War II that the white Cinderella fantasy dress came into the price range of our ancestors.

Tradition would be a Wednesday-night wedding in October. Americans lived on farms and small towns, and fall was the only time when agricultural communities could spare the money and the time from the grim business of staying alive.

Tradition would be one attendant and a short guest list. Everybody in town may have been invited, but there were only a hundred citizens back then. Elopements were common when the consent of the father mattered more than the consent of the daughter.

Even brides have changed as each generation demands different things from women. You don't have to be a cultural historian to know that brides are no longer judged on their ability to sit out a prairie blizzard in a sod hut, nor on their skill in making felt and sequin telephone-book covers. Brides who cooked everything from scratch bore daughters who made TV dinners and granddaughters who pop everything into the microwave.

The way brides and grooms interact hasn't changed throughout history, but the way brides and their times have interacted certainly has. Let's take a look at how weddings – and brides – have changed since the start of the century.

1904: *Home on the Range in a Sod Hut*

Axel and Fredricka Strehlau (née Bremer) were married at Kadoka, South Dakota, after a courtship by mail. Axel had a small ranch outside Kadoka for twelve years before he felt need of a wife. He sent several letters to his home village in Germany in search of a wife willing to move to the prairie, but none were answered, so he joined an American pen-pal club and proposed to three women within six months. It was Fredricka who accepted, and a grateful Axel immediately bought and sent her a train ticket from Maine to Kadoka.

After they were married, they lived in Axel's sod hut until he was able to build a wooden frame house. Fredricka never went up to the second story of that house because the view it offered – the bleakness of the prairie and the badlands in the distance – made her swoon.

Fredricka had been born and raised in New England, and although she dearly loved her husband, she often asked God why he had punished her by sending her to a land without trees.

Axel was proud of the flat and desolate
land. It was his.

There were seven major blizzards
the first winter in that sod hut, but
only once when they couldn't open
the door against the drifted snow.

Number of guests at wedding: The Kadoka station master agreed to witness the wedding when the bride arrived from the East.

Number of attendants: The station master's daughter, the station master's wife and the minister's wife all joined in.

Special reading: The Kadoka station master had his eye on the territorial statehouse, so he made a stem-winder of a speech, which nobody remembered, except that it was long.

Highlight of the wedding party: The party had to be cut short because it looked like a storm was coming in off the badlands.

Favorite wedding gift: The local doctor gave them three chickens, which had been his pay for delivering a baby that morning.

Honeymoon: Five years later, Axel and Fredricka were able to spend four days with Axel's sister at her ranch outside of Hettinger, North Dakota.

1922: Careless Youth in an Age of Normalcy

*N*an would have been the first to tell you that she was not a Flapper. In her crowd, the women were referred to as Shebas and the men as Sheiks. To be a Flapper was, well, a little low rent. Sheiks and Shebas entertained with smuggled gin instead of that mixture of near-beer and wood alcohol known as South Dakota champagne.

Nan grew up in as progressive an environment as her father's Presbyterian principles would allow, but she was continually shocking the poor man, rejecting everything that was not "modern" or "scientific." Cubist paintings were properly modern. Freud was both modern and scientific. Her parents' prairie Presbyterian precepts were neither modern nor scientific to Nan's mind.

With her mother's tacit encouragement, Nan became active in Margaret Sanger's eugenic birth-control movement, risking arrest (and her father's fear of public humiliation) by passing out birth-control information on streetcars.

Nan met Roger at a rally for Sacco and Vanzetti, and they hit it off immediately. Within a month, Roger had quit his job at the bank and they had moved to Greenwich Village, where he undertook to become a major free-verse poet.

Her own artistic ambitions awakened, Nan caused quite a scandal back home when word leaked out that she had been posing in the nude for a famous and openly lesbian Polish sculptress.

In an unexpected display of filial piety, Nan and Roger returned home long enough to get married in her home church, even though the minister was troubled by their way of life. Nan's father was triumphant because appearances had been restored.

Number of guests at wedding: Seventy-five.

Number of attendants: Four.

Special reading: Nan's greatest ambition was to have Dorothy Parker say something wittily nasty about her. Finally, Parker obliged, saying of Nan:

> She's one of nature's masterpieces–
> Odd how soon her fascination ceases.

Highlight of the wedding party: Nan's grandmother told her that she had been arrested in 1890 while campaigning for women's suffrage and that her minister had denounced her anti-family behavior from the pulpit.

Favorite wedding gift: Nan's father gave them a ticket to Paris, figuring that if they were going to live scandalously, they might as well do it where nobody in her hometown would know.

Honeymoon: They stayed in Paris for 18 months, considering every minute of it a honeymoon.

1943: GI Joe Meets Rosie the Riveter

Marcus first saw Sadie when the Zion Choir came to Corinthian Baptist Church for an evening of fellowship and gospel singing. Sadie paid him no attention, but when he showed up at Zion Baptist the next Wednesday for the prayer meeting, she managed to sit nearby. Within a month they were going to movies on Saturday night, and it wasn't too much longer before Sadie was getting up to get second helpings for Marcus at church dinners.

Her parents liked him. She liked him and she thought it was sweet when he got tongue tied around her. She liked to listen to him imitate movie stars. She even liked to listen to him practice his saxophone, no matter how badly he played. He liked her and he liked her parents and he liked to make her laugh.

The war changed their lives.

Marcus wanted to go fight "Mr. Adolf" face to face. Sadie knew all about duty, but she wished Marcus would turn just a little lame. He surprised everyone by up and enlisting one day, but before he left, he proposed. Sadie accepted.

They planned to have a big wedding during Marcus's two-week leave after boot camp, but when his orders were changed, they held a small ceremony in her parents' living room instead.

Reverend Nesbitt said they should have faith in God's protection; Aunt Senora played "I Love You Truly," "Because" and "The Lord's Prayer," and everybody sang along. Properly married, Marcus left to catch the troop train.

Far from liberating Europe singlehandedly, Marcus spent his service coordinating USO tours and playing dance music for troops shipping out to the front. Sadie got a job rewinding electrical motors at the new war plant in town. She sent some money to her sisters and her parents, but mostly she saved, and her nest egg helped her and Marcus get on their feet after the war.

Although Sadie read Marcus's letters daily and put his ring back on as soon as she left the war plant, she didn't really feel married till she stood with him at his homecoming party in the basement of Zion Baptist and heard Reverend Nesbitt say a prayer thanking the Lord that Marcus had been restored to them. The women had cooked greens and ham and fried chicken and sweet potatoes and corn bread and cakes three layers thick and everything else you couldn't get in the army. Everyone ate till they couldn't stand it and talked among each other for hours and then went home, leaving Marcus and Sadie to restart their lives.

Number of guests at wedding: Only nine relatives could make it on such short notice, which was all the living room could hold anyway.

Number of attendants: Sadie's sister was matron of honor and Marcus's brother stood up for him.

Special reading: The newspaper that day was encouraging, suggesting that the war would soon be over and our boys would soon be home, safe with their families.

Highlight of the wedding party: Sadie was grateful that no one cried, because she knew that she could not have controlled herself had she started to cry.

Favorite wedding gift: They were hoping for a deep-fat fryer, but appliances were in short supply for the duration. Sadie treasured an embroidered pillow cover Marcus sent home from London, even if it did say "Mother."

Honeymoon: Immediately after the wedding, Marcus went to Greenland, Iceland, England, France, Switzerland, Austria, Germany and Fort Sill, Oklahoma. Sadie went back to work. After the war, they took the train to Chicago for two days.

Sadie was delighted when Marcus was sent to Officers Candidate School because it meant that nobody would be shooting at him. They wrote each other often – cheerful, guarded letters that bolstered their spirits and gave no voice to the fear and loneliness that dominated their lives.

1957: Tammy Marries Davy Crockett

As far as Arlene was concerned, the fifties were just about perfect. She loved the clothes – cashmere sweaters were very flattering to the well-endowed young miss – and she loved the exuberance of the times, where one fun fad, like Davy Crockett, was followed by another, like hula hoops, that was even more fun.

It was a time of community, with something for everyone to join – Great Books Clubs, Craft Clubs, Community Concerts and church guilds. Even career girls had their own club. There was always something happening, like neighborhood picnics that everybody attended (except those far-out eggheads on the corner), class trips and sock hops for students and hayrides sponsored by the Miss Junior Jaycees.

But then, Arlene was in love with Bob, and a girl with stars in her eyes certainly sees things through rose-colored glasses. She loved rubbing Butch-wax into Bob's flat-top, she loved the smell of his Old Spice, and she knew she was just going to love, love, love being married to him. She knew she wanted lots of kids and she already had the first two names chosen. Bob Jr. would be first, of course, and she'd call her little girl MeloDee.

Bob was ready to settle down after college and his two years in the army. He was eager to get into a grey flannel suit and start his career in advertising. The army had taught him how to get along with the guys and to watch out for anyone who was too "far out" because he might be a "fellow traveler." Bob thought it was a sign of good civic hygiene that four out of five Americans were ready to inform the FBI of any relatives or neighbors whose politics were suspect. "Community" to Bob meant that there were standards that we all accepted, and anyone who refused to conform should be watched.

Arlene and Bob lived in separate but equal worlds. Bob's world was his all-chrome Oldsmobile and his chrome-metal office tower downtown. Arlene's world was her new split-level home, fully equipped with all the chrome-plated household gadgets her little heart could desire. Both did their part to keep the economy booming: She was an expert shopper, and he taught manufacturers the value of planned obsolescence.

Their wedding was one the Joneses could only *dream* about keeping up with. Arlene's dress was a tulle cloud, and she had an unheard-of four attendants! All of Bob and Arlene's fathers' business associates, all the relatives, all the neighbors and everybody's friends were there. More than 400 people crammed into The Cat 'n' the Fiddle Supper Club for the reception, and if it hadn't been for her tranquilizers, Arlene's mom would have jumped right out of her skin.

Both her veil and her identity were blown away within half an hour on Arlene's wedding day.

Sister Rose of the Sorrows cracked everybody up when she tried the hula-hoop.

Arlene had frankly expected more when she dragged Bob to the Greenwich Village beatnik hangout. There was some dirty guy reading dirty poetry, people who snapped their fingers instead of clapping and a not-very-polite waitress who chain-smoked.

Number of guests at wedding: 453.

Number of attendants: Eight.

Special reading: The homily was based on *The Power of Positive Thinking*, and the priest concluded by saying, "To get along with God, go along with God. Be God's kind of guy!"

Highlight of the wedding party: Sister Rose of the Sorrows, Arlene's favorite parochial-school teacher, sent everybody into hysterics when she tried to do the hula-hoop.

Favorite wedding gift: Along with all the other wonderful gifts, everybody brought "Stock-a-Shelter" supplies – radiation detectors, dried and canned food, sealed drinking water, fresh batteries and utility candles for the H-bomb shelter Bob was planning to build behind their new split-level.

Honeymoon: The honeymoon was as grand as the wedding. Bob and Arlene went to New York for a week, tried to get tickets to *My Fair Lady* but only managed *Li'l Abner*. Then they flew to Jamaica, where Bob drank rum all week instead of dry martinis and they both learned how to do the limbo, although Bob fell down a lot more than Arlene did.

1969: Living in the Age of Aquariums

Marcie met Randy at a fraternity mixer in 1965, where Randy's band (known as Randy and the Rovers) was trying to get through "Louie, Louie" for the fourteenth time that night. Within a few months they were considered "an item" by Marcie's friends in nursing school, all of whom expected her to get pinned before Christmas.

Concern among her friends grew when Marcie let her subscriptions to both *Seventeen* and *Cosmopolitan* lapse. When she started reading Ferlinghetti instead of Rod McKuen, the girls considered calling her parents.

Randy dropped his major in economics, started taking theater classes, then apprenticed himself to a boat builder. He continued to play in his old band, now renamed The Electric Raspberry, until some fraternity boys beat him unconscious when he tried to play a sitar at homecoming.

To nurse him back to health, Marcie moved onto the farm Randy had rented thirty-seven miles outside the city. He had found the farm by casting the I Ching, and took delight in its thirty acres of woods, its stream and the beaver pond.

They lived there for four years, hosting a colorful series of guests ranging from the musician who was nearly arrested by the local sheriff (who thought it suspicious that a Chicago resident would have Illinois license plates on his car), to the Berry Queen, a woman who had moved to a Mexican fishing village in 1959 and was now getting ironically rich exporting Mexican wedding shirts to head shops in the United States.

To atone for all the fun they were having, they endured the curiosity of a young professor in the university's anthropology department, who treated Marcie, Randy and their "tribe" as if he had discovered the world's last (unstudied) primitives.

When Marcie's father threatened to swear out an arrest warrant for cohabitation (a felony with a penalty of three years' imprisonment), Marcie and Randy agreed to get married, but on their land and with their friends – at dawn.

Aunt Joan fainted dead away when she saw the bouquet.

Marcie's mother, Clarice, was outraged that her daughter wanted to "do her own thing." Clarice believed that Marcie owed her this wedding. Clarice had been forced to do *her* mother's thing at her own wedding, and she damned well planned to do her thing this time. Instead, Marcie was planning a happening. Clarice had no idea what happened at a happening, but she was certain that she would disapprove.

Lynn, AP and KB, three of Marcie's friends who were into cooking, catered the affair and threw in some magic muffins as their own wedding gift. The invitation was a psychedelic silkscreen poster that may or may not have been a photograph of Marcie and Randy in the nude. It was sort of hard to tell, particularly for the relatives with bifocals. Bleary-eyed in the dawn, the relatives all came to make sure the wedding was grimly legal, and were offended by nearly everything they saw. Marcie had put big white bows on all the sheep, geese and pigs, and the barnyard dog was rigged with a harness to serve as the flower dog.

Aunt Joan (a religious woman always on the lookout for Satan's sins of sensuality) fainted dead away when she saw the bridal bouquet made of carrots. It was phallic, but it was sort of funny, everybody else agreed.

Marcie's father was relieved to find no North Vietnamese flags in evidence, although he did look around for them a bit. Not too much, really, just a quick peek under a few beds and in the hayloft.

Several years later, Marcie and Randy drove to Las Vegas to be married legally. The "minister" who had conducted the meadow ceremony was a friend famous for his "Duroc Gold" – a potent cannabis grown in his former hog pen. He had a resonant voice and was graying at the temples, and in Marcie's family, qualities like that were synonymous with righteousness. Her parents never once suspected that they'd been had.

Number of guests at wedding: Fifty-five, including the photographer and reporter from *Life* magazine who camped out in the nuptial meadow to get the story.
Number of attendants: Four. There were going to be, like, nine, but dawn is such a time bummer, you know.
Special reading: The whole wedding was taken out of Kahlil Gibran, except for the vows, which Randy and Marcie wrote themselves.
Highlight of the wedding party: After the Republican relatives had fled in horror, the entire wedding party went skinny-dipping in the beaver pond. They got mellow, blew soap bubbles and asked each other whether they had ever, you know, really *looked* at their hands...
Favorite wedding gift: A sitar that this really close friend of Dylan's once had and Randy tried to learn, but then decided to do something else instead.
Honeymoon: Randy and Marcie bought a 30-day bus pass to go search for America.

1976: *The Bicentennial Disco*

*I*f Pat hadn't been thrown off that mechanical bucking bull, she never would have met Don at the Chiropractic Wellness Clinic. Don had what he liked to call tennis elbow, although he had only hurt his arm falling off his moped.

Don was a man of a thousand styles. He had shirts whose collars nearly touched his shoulders and shirts that unbuttoned to the belt. He had gold chains and some hair on his chest. He walked on elevator shoes so high they had goldfish in their Lucite heels, and he could swagger in cowboy boots like the best dime-store cowboy alive. He had polyester disco pants that flared but never ripped, designer jeans that hugged his tight little butt and an entire suburban Superfly ensemble.

Pat liked diversity in a man. She herself could change in a moment's notice from Laura Ashley to pantsuits to disco to urban cowgirl. Pat got a lot of her dates through the personal columns, and it was always tough to keep things both appropriate and novel. It was time for them to settle down. She was tired of wearing eye makeup to aerobics classes, and he was tired of sucking in his stomach when he played racquetball with blind dates. In short, they were getting bored with an era whose most conspicuous sex symbol was Henry Kissinger.

They fell in love on the disco floor. Pat was awed by how Don moved his body just like John Travolta in *Saturday Night Fever*. Don loved watching Pat dance and told her that she looked just like what's-her-name who starred opposite Travolta.

Pat gave her mother complete control over the wedding, and her mother went happily berserk. All Pat remembers of the day (or night) was the disco reception. The local paper did a full-page article about it in the Lifestyle section, and *People* magazine sent a photographer. "It was my girlhood dream," sighed Pat. "No more dating and no more worrying about herpes!"

Pat was into macramé in a big way. She even macramaéd herself a dress, which she never wore because she could never find her body stocking.

Don had nine cowboy hats, one for each leisure suit. His favorite was the hat with the whole pheasant butt on the front.

Number of guests at wedding: 250

Number of attendants: Twelve.

Special reading: The maid of honor sang a selection of passages from *I'm OK, You're OK!* set to Cat Stevens music as Don and Pat exchanged matching mood rings.

Highlight of the wedding party: A forty-minute solo dance by the bride and groom that everybody really, really loved.

Favorite wedding gift: The women in Pat's consciousness raising group chipped in for a mirrored ball to hang in the bedroom, to "honor Pat's growing self-discovery and awareness of the power potentialities of her body."

Honeymoon: They booked a disco cruise to six ports from Florida to Louisiana. It was such a Dance-O-Rama that they seldom even went ashore to explore these exotic locations.

1985: The Power Wedding

*D*exter and Nina perfectly embodied the 1980s emphasis on return to traditional values, embracing tradition with such fervor as to suggest that they believed they had invented it. Emphatic that they were not the shallow "experience seekers" of the sixties and seventies, Dex and Nina lived their lives "following their gut," not "going with the flow."

As Dex put it: "We do what we do because we can do it. Or rather, because we *can* do it. We work hard for our money and there's no reason we should be ashamed that we're well compensated."

Dex made his reputation and achieved some significant financial independence presenting his seminar, "Employee Benefits Versus Prosperity: Your Choice!" to Fortune 500 companies around the country. Nina began her career as a systems analyst for a junk-bond house, then left to start a consulting firm called Trusted Servant, which provided a full array of employee monitoring technology, from Deskside Infrared heat sensors and computer keystroke review to phone monitoring and hidden video cameras.

For their wedding, Dex and Nina flew their families, the minister and eight attendants each to Hawaii, where they were married at a friend's estate. They left immediately for an around-the-world honeymoon, during which they were remarried by a Shinto priest in Japan and again by one of the Dalai Lama's assistants in Tibet. In India, they had a Hindu wedding ceremony atop an elephant, and in Cairo had their marriage blessed by a Muslim cleric. The simple but elegant reaffirmation of their vows in a quaint chapel in the shadow of the Vatican meant a lot to Nina, and the view was breathtaking when they were remarried in the Swiss Alps by a Calvinist minister. Understandably, they took the honeymoon suite in Paris at the Hotel Georges V, and were remarried for the final time in Westminster Cathedral in London.

"We really believe in tradition," declared Dexter. "We see our weddings as the synthesis of every major religious tradition that has survived in the marketplace of ideas."

Dexter demonstrated the trickle-down theory to his guests with $145 a bottle champagne.

Dexter and Nina hoped to have more quality time for each other on their honeymoon, but they had to tie up a few loose ends first.

Number of guests at original wedding: 150.
Number of attendants: Sixteen.
Special reading: Nina read from Nancy Reagan's interview in which she said she loved her husband so much that she ate bananas (which she disliked) in bed rather than crackers so the crunching wouldn't keep "Daddy" awake.
Highlight of the wedding party: When they dimmed the lights (it was a night wedding), Nina appeared in a dress with 1,000 faux pearls, 2,400 sequins and 500 tiny battery-powered twinkle lights sewn into it. It was to die for.

Favorite wedding gift: Although Dex and Nina were listed on thirty-nine computerized gift registries, totaling 462 pages of gift needs, they were particularly fond of the $775 (each) china place settings for eighteen, the eighteen settings of crystal (including white wine, red wine, water, champagne and sherbet pieces each at $175 a stem), the $1,495 silver settings for eighteen, the complete Nautilus gym, the designer ski ensembles and all five of the $1,000 gift certificates to The Sharper Image.
Honeymoon: Dex had their vacation videotapes professionally edited (with a score and soundtrack added), then made 250 copies and sent them in lieu of thank-you notes.

1992: *Eco-ing out an Existence, or "My Kind of Gaia"*

*K*ris and Jim no longer want it all. They just want safe sex, safe sun and safety belts in their car. They also want to save the rain forest, save the ozone layer, save the spotted owl, save the wetlands and save the family farm. Although Kris couldn't save her first marriage and Jim couldn't save his old job at the S&L, they did manage to save their dignity and sanity (as well as their savings accounts) by moving in together and deciding to get married.

It would be safe to say that Tasha and Zach thought it was a great idea. Tasha, aged twelve, and Zach, age ten, were Kris's kids, and they had suffered along with their mother through a succession of highly unsuitable suitors in the three years since she had divorced their father, Jeffrey, who, at age thirty-nine, had bought a red Porsche and then gone slightly girl-crazy. The hormonal tempest was just too much for the poor dear.

Kris and Jim met at her work when he was transferred to her department as an accounting temp. Jim always had been crazy about women who used cruelty-free cosmetics, and they really hit it off when she brought him chemical-free strawberries as they brown-bagged it in the cafeteria.

Despite the protests of her mother, Kris announced that she planned to be married on the banks of the Apple River by a shaman-healer named Dancing Buffalo, who was known as Melissa Kaplan when she and Kris were roommates at the university. After the wedding and reception, Kris, Jim, Tasha and Zach made their getaway by tubing down the Apple River.

The wedding was planned as a model of conspicuous nonconsumption and respect for the world's resources. Kris got an elegant beaded lace gown for $10 at Ragstock, which is where Jim got the white swallowtail tux coats for himself and Zach. There were no matching pants available, but that was OK since they could wear their bathing suits. After all, it would look silly to wear a full tuxedo into the water.

One of the men on the eco-tour worked for NASA and handed out space-shuttle brochures to all the villagers in the Amazon.

Number of guests at wedding: Twenty-seven.
Number of attendants: Rather than waste resources on dresses that could be worn only once, Kris asked every woman at the wedding to serve as a joy-bringer to her marriage vows.
Special reading: The shaman-healer who married Kris and Jim gave them a special prayer, printed on bark (taken from a naturally deceased tree): "Visualize the inner child of your adult child as a spiritual warrior, walking in balance and holistic harmony with the earth mother. Then let your inner child heal the negative energy in your chakras and tear down your dysfunctional boundaries. Bond to your partner, but be independent, not codependent. Know that the path of the wise leads one always to be a facilitator, but not an enabler. Seek serenity and give good strokes. Be wise."

Highlight of the wedding party: During the Permaculture portion of the wedding preparations, they sowed both heirloom and traditional seeds in their back yard and had a Chinese geomancer determine a propitious location to plant a hardy tree. The wedding music was supplied by Jim's men's group, who played Moroccan flutes and a ceremonial drum brought back from Papua New Guinea.
Favorite wedding gift: Even though Uncle Vern believed that anyone not married by a Lutheran minister was on shaky theological grounds, he gave them a fully stocked tool kit and the complete Time-Life Home Repair series.
Honeymoon: With all the money they saved by hosting a sensible wedding, Kris and Jim splurged on an eco-tour to the Amazon rain forest, where everybody shared stories of their past life regressions and where Kris taught Aurora, the camp cook, the basic principles of reflexology.

After a brief reception Kris, Jim, Tasha and Zach, made their getaway on tubes down the Apple River, followed by most of the guests in their own tubes.

A Thank-You Note

I hadn't realized that I'd turned into an old duffer until I started to write this book. That's when I noticed how few of my close personal friends were twenty years old. But I've wanted to do a wedding parody ever since I worked at a studio in high school, so I did my homework and got up to speed on weddings in the nineties. Along the way, I met some wonderful folks and was reminded how much courage it takes to get married in an uncertain world.

The most important person in my work on this book is, was and ever shall be my own bride, Adaire Colleen Peterson. After eighteen years of behaving like newlyweds, we see no reason to grow up now. Our wedding was a gas! The photos were taken by the best man, Raymond Elisha Chesnut III, a former combat photographer in Vietnam. Ray got great pictures and never once lifted his head. Chris Burling, who is arguably both Adaire's and my best friend, stood up for us. Family and friends crammed into a little Lutheran chapel for the wedding and then adjoined to the Fellowship Hall (it was a new church, so there was no basement) for ham sandwiches and chocolate cake.

By contrast, I figure we staged the equivalent of nine full weddings to produce the photographs for this book. The Carlson family has gone beyond the call of duty in helping. Bonnie Carlson, the world's greatest seamstress and model, helped with so many dresses I lost count. Daughter Susan Anderson brought along four of her wedding attendants (Cecelia Duncan, Marsha Aspelund, Chris Poole and sister Beret Carlson) to stage Marc and Missi's wedding album. Her hubby, Jeff Anderson, brother Scott Carlson and niece Thea Fuller were in the wedding party as well. Dave Bell was the lucky groom. The other folks in the album are Carl Schmidt, Terry Bartlett Jr., Mark Anderson, Donna Anderson, Robert Bledsoe, Marlin Bree, Althea Dixon, Laura Gingras, Kathryn Goffin, the bouquet-catching Sara Grady, Jeanette, Gus and Drew Johnson, John and Kathy Lenartz, and Lennis Carpentier, who is legally required to appear in all my books. We shot at the Riverwood Conference Center, Cheryl Neisen assisted and the wedding cake was created by Carol Paal. Aljohn's Beach Shop supplied the classy shades.

The Brides through the Ages presented some tremendous challenges, and I wouldn't have been able to meet them without Tessie Bundick, a wonder-woman who did all the costumes, make-up and hair. Keith Zolinski was of invaluable assistance here and in photo shootings throughout the book. For the 1904 shoot at Interior, South Dakota, when we needed a chicken wrangler, Jean Amiotte was there. Julie and Andy Riedlinger were our couple at the Prairie Homestead wearing costumes from Chanhassen Dinner Theater. Craig Naaken allowed us to photograph the Dakota shield. Dondee Krolikowski really is a superwoman. She enjoys her work; she's got a wonderful hubby, Jeff, and a great family; she's hospitable and makes great chili; and to top it off, she's a rodeo star.

The paper moon was made by Ready, Set, Go. Tessie made the gown and located the authentic 1920s tux for Christine Gough and Tom Hense, who were the thoroughly modern couple. Marc Carter wore a uniform from Doug Bekke's collection and Wanda Williams was outfitted, wigged and made-up by Tessie (of course) and Via's for the melancholy 1943 series.

Brad Horten actually got a 1950s crewcut for the 1957 shot and it didn't ruin his reputation at work! Suzanne Carter spent a day having her veil and dress "fly away," courtesy of Tessie and Keith. Molly Grady isn't really a beatnik, even though she sometimes dresses all in black. Jo Lynne Hook is no nun, and she never dresses in black. Peter Linnes-Bagley is wearing the little suit my mother saved. Palm Brothers supplied the table and restaurant ware, and Judy Olausen's studio certainly does look like it could host a poetry reading.

Allison Hoekstra and Max Johnson make wonderful flower children, even if they were only sprouts during the sixties, and Dayle and Marge Erickson make an imposing couple with their ribboned pup, Muffin Peterson. Annmarie Griffiths and Colin Kegel Jr. can get behind the idea that they're all right and you're all right, even if they don't really dance beneath DB Sound's lights or wear Benson Optical half-tinted shades. Beth Johnson at Minnesota Jet was certainly a godsend, making the jet for the power wedding available to Beth Chaplin and Mark Mills. Martha at Holm & Olson made up their fine and trendy bouquet; Surdyk's supplied the mega-expensive champagne bottle; and Beth pumped up at Scanticon under the personal training of Scott Elvrum.

Linda Sorenson doesn't swim, so what was she doing floating down the Apple River at Terrace Tubes in Somerset, Wisconsin? Praying, I assume. Bill Wickmann does swim, however, as do Adam and Anna Witt, the remainder of their blended nineties family.

Other folks have gone to great lengths for this book – hanging upside down, like Lori Hansen (who was "flown" by Bruce Allen), or diving near nurse sharks and barracuda like Julissa Zabodeh, a fantastic diver and Miss Orange Walk of Belize. In alphabetical order, I'd like to thank each and every one of these folks. They are: Rick Bancroft, Bingo the Clown, Jim Church, Jim Cutrara, Carrie Daklin, Lori

Edwardsen, Annie & Katie Foss, Nan Gianolli, Jim Haider, Jenna Klein, Peggy Krenik, Karna M. Lehr, Hugh Madson, Bryan Martin, Jim Martin, Marty Miller, Jeffrey L. Nelson, Chris Norris, Mark Patzloff, Bjorn Peterson, Eric Peterson, Michele Regnier, Charlotte Richards, Carl Schmidt, Kim Steidmeyer, Kathy and Randall Solem, Debbie Warner, Peggy Wilson, Margaret Woodburn, Lisa Utrik and Amy Zinschlag.

What would a wedding be without flowers? More specifically, where would I have been without 38th Street Flowers, who turned out bouquet after bouquet and kept their humor? And what would I have done without Bobbie D. Carter at Formal Affair and their tuxedos? Trudie Blumentritt was awfully generous in loaning us her wedding album knowing that our perfect god-daughters, Marit and Rachel Peterson, would be laughing at it. Elda of Elda Victoriana Dolls made the beautiful bride and groom puppets and Bob Ritchie's beautiful old car now has a beautiful young leg sticking out of it. Margaret Harpestad makes wonderful Barbie Doll bridal gowns, sells them all over southern Minnesota and doesn't charge enough for them. We appreciate being able to shoot at Hamline University stadium, the Chanhassen Bowl and Tom & Terry Polski's house. Tom Casmer came through again with an angelic design for the Post-it note and Elizabeth Helmes created that beautiful recycled-materials wedding dress.

Sylvia Paine is not only the world's greatest editor, she's the world's most patient editor, having put up with me for three books now. I have learned a great deal from her. Tim Morse and Julie Szamocki at Yamamoto Moss did a fantastic design job on this book. I'm awed by their creativity and skill, to say nothing of Tim's collection of wristwatches. Doug Bekke is the magician who supplied the retouching magic, for which I am most grateful.

Jim Martin of Gopher State Litho has been my account exec, printing guru, occasional model, prop master and all-round facilitator now since *Scandinavian Humor* in 1986. And the amazing thing is that Nick Ketz, the owner of Gopher State, allows this sort of thing to go on! I'm lucky to have fallen in with them and their talented crew.

I am profoundly grateful to the radiant Mary Hart, who so generously offered the introduction to this book. Thanks, Mary! It meant a lot to me.

These are the folks who made this book possible. My thanks and my gratitude go out to everyone, named and unnamed, who went beyond the call of duty to help make this book happen.

JOHN LOUIS ANDERSON
Taking pictures at his own wedding, September 7, 1974.

Know somebody going through or recovering from a wedding? Share the fun of Off The Bridal Path with your friends!

Mail to: **Nordbook** P.O. Box 249 Chaska, MN 55318
Or Fax to: **(612) 448-5011**

Only $19.45 (Mailing and handling included)
Minnesota Residents please add 6% sales tax

I have enclosed $_____ for _____ books.

Name _____

Address _____

City/State _____ Zip _____

✂ ···

Mail to: **Nordbook** P.O. Box 249 Chaska, MN 55318
Or Fax to: **(612) 448-5011**

Only $19.45 (Mailing and handling included)
Minnesota Residents please add 6% sales tax

I have enclosed $_____ for _____ books.

Name _____

Address _____

City/State _____ Zip _____